The *South Beach* method for Conversational Italian

By: Erasmus-Cromwell Smith

ISBN: 979-8-9866136-2-8

Publisher: Erasmus Press
Editor and Proofreading: Elisa Arraiz Lucca
Cover Design and Interior Design: Abjini Shamanik
www.erasmuscromwellsmith.com

This course is radically different from any others as you will be taking steps backwards to revisit a bit of English Grammar in order to refresh certain rules and practices of our language.

As you will see, there are plenty of things we say simply because we are used to but on many of them, we don't know whether they are right or even why we speak that way.

The premise is simple, we go back and revisit our language to refresh or learn certain concepts to translate English properly into Italian. Our own language construction has to be grammatically right (properly built), otherwise what will come out in Italian will be equally wrong!

Conversational Italian

- This course will enable you to speak Italian within hours.

- This course debunks the idea that Italian is a very hard language to learn.

- Actually, in most cases, both languages are spoken in the same way (literally like a mirror image).

- The Foundation of this method is the Infinitive Verbs.

- You will learn to speak through 4 templates (all of them using Infinitive Verbs).

- The method also teaches you how to pronounce/spell properly in Italian.

- It also allows/enables you to study/learn most Italian Verbs only in Infinitive Form (almost without conjugations) effectively cutting thousands of hours and thousands of verb conjugations from the learning process.

Italian is an EASY language to LEARN as it is to SPEAK

Let Us Begin...

For the most part :

- Italian is spoken the same way English is!

- Most of the grammar rules (even their names) are the same.

- Phrases are structured the same way.

- Many, many words are very similar if not the same.

Italian difficulty debunked:

Italian vowels have only one sound:

English has two or more sounds per vowel!

So, let's debunk the idea that Italian is so difficult!

Learning Step 1

Everything Begins With

The 5 Vowels

Next you will learn how to pronounce them easily!

The Basics First : "The Vowels"

Italian Vowel	Italian Pronunciation	Easy: Pronunciation is in parenthesis ( )			
A (AH) Read Aloud	Again **Ah**	Again **Ah**	Again **Ah**	Again **Ah**
E (EH)	**Eh**	**Eh**	**Eh**	**Eh**
I (EE)	**Ee**	**Ee**	**Ee**	**Ee**
O (OH)	**Oh**	**Oh**	**Oh**	**Oh**
U (OO)	**Ooh**	**Ooh**	**Ooh**	**Ooh**

Now let's practice them one after the other: **AH-EH-EE-OH-OOH**

Now do it faster: **AH-EH-EE-OH-OOH**   now even faster: **AH-EH-EE-OH-OOH**

Keep on practicing: **AH-EH-EE-OH-OOH**   until you memorize it

Repeat and memorize the sound. **AH-EH-EE-OH-OOH**

Try to do it faster & faster.

Learning Step 2

Next is to learn

The Alphabet

Pronunciation in Italian is in (parenthesis)!

Pronunciation and phonetics of the Italian Alphabet

A (ah)	B (bee)	C (chee)	D (dee)	E (eh)	F (eh-ffeh)
G (gee)	H (ah-kkah)	I (ee)	J (*)	K (*)	L (eh-lleh)
M (eh-mmeh)	N (eh-nnen)	O (oh)	P (pee)	Q (koo)	R (eh-rreh)
S (eh-sseh)	T (tee)	U (ooh)	V (voo)	W (*)	
X (*)	Y (*)	Z (zeh-tah)			

(*) the letters J, K, W, X, Y do not exist in the Italian language.

Learning Step 2

It is also very useful to learn

The Numbers

Uno	Due	Tre	Quattro	Cinque	Sei	Sette	Otto	Nove
One	Two	Three	Four	Five	Six	Seven	Eight	Nine
Dieci	Venti	Trenta	Quaranta	Cinquanta	Sessanta	Settanta	Ottanta	Novanta
Ten	Twenty	Thirty	Forty	Fifty	Sixty	Seventy	Eighty	Ninety

Cento One hundred	**Duecento** Two hundred	**Trecento** Three hundred	**Quattrocento** Four hundred
Cinquecento Five hundred	**Seicento** Six hundred	**Settecento** Seven hundred	**Ottocento** Eight hundred
Novecento Nine hundred	**Mille** One thousand	**Diecimila** Ten thousand	**Centomila** One hundred thousand
Un milione One million	**Cento milioni** One hundred million	**Un miliardo** One billion	**Mille miliardi** One trillion

Learning Step 3

Having learned the alphabet and the vowels, the next step is to learn:

The Nouns

I - You	Easy, just read it! ()
Read it aloud	Read it aloud
I – IO (ee-oh)	You – TU (too)
Read it aloud	Read it aloud
I - IO	You – TU
Read it aloud	Read it aloud
I - IO	You – TU
Read it aloud	Read it aloud
I - IO	You – TU
Read it aloud	Read it aloud
I - IO	You – TU
Read it aloud	Read it aloud
I - IO	You – TU
Read it aloud	Read it aloud
I - IO	You – TU
Read it aloud	Read it aloud
I - IO	You – TU

Remember in Italian I is IO, You is TU

He - She   Easy , just read it ! ()

Read it aloud	Read it aloud
He – LUI (loo-ee)	She – LEI (leh-ee)

Read it aloud	Read it aloud
He - LUI	She – LEI

Read it aloud	Read it aloud
He - LUI	She – LEI

Read it aloud	Read it aloud
He - LUI	She – LEI

Read it aloud	Read it aloud
He - LUI	She – LEI

Read it aloud	Read it aloud
He - LUI	She – LEI

Read it aloud	Read it aloud
He - LUI	She – LEI

Read it aloud	Read it aloud
He - LUI	She – LEI

Remember in Italian He is LUI , She is LEI

We - You   Easy , just read it ! ()

Read it aloud	Read it aloud
We – NOI (noh-ee)	You – VOI (voh-ee)
Read it aloud	Read it aloud
We - NOI	You – VOI
Read it aloud	Read it aloud
We - NOI	You – VOI
Read it aloud	Read it aloud
We - NOI	You – VOI
Read it aloud	Read it aloud
We - NOI	You – VOI
Read it aloud	Read it aloud
We - NOI	You – VOI
Read it aloud	Read it aloud
We - NOI	You – VOI
Read it aloud	Read it aloud
We - NOI	You – VOI

Remember in Italian <u>We</u> is NOI, <u>You</u> is VOI

They - It   Easy , just read it ! ()

Read it aloud

They – LORO (loh-roh)

Read it aloud

It (*)

Read it aloud

They - LORO

Read it aloud

They - LORO

Read it aloud

They - LORO

Read it aloud

They - LORO

Read it aloud

They - LORO

Read it aloud

They - LORO

Remember in Italian <u>They</u> is LORO, <u>It</u> is usually omitted

(*) usually omitted, colloquially speaking

SUMMARY	**The Nouns**	Easy, just read it! ()
Let's continue to practice!	I - IO (ee-oh)	Repeat it 5 times!
	You – Tu (too)	Repeat it 5 times!
	He - LUI (loo-ee)	Repeat 5 more times
	She - LEI (leh-ee).	This one 5 times as well
	We - NOI (noh-ee)	Pronounce this one 5 times
	You - VOI (voh-ee)	This one 5 times as well
	They - LORO (loh-roh) this as well	5 times with
	(*) «It» is usually omitted, colloquially speaking	

Learning Step 4

The following are essential to any conversation:

Magic Words

Practice them!

Let us introduce a few words that are essential in any conversation

An/A	=	Un, uno, una	Yes	=	Sì
			No	=	No
The	=	Il, lo, la, I, gli, le	At	=	A, in
With	=	Con	That	=	Quello/quella/quel
And	=	E	To	=	A
Or	=	O	This	=	Questo/questa

What	=	Cosa	But	=	Ma
When	=	Quando	Whose	=	Di chi
Where	=	Dove	Who	=	Chi
Why/Because	=	Perché	Which	=	Quale
Whether	=	Se	How	=	Come
To	=	A	For	=	Per
From	=	Da	While	=	Mentre
How Many	=	Quanti	Whom	=	Cui
For	=	Per	As	=	Come
More than	=	Più di	How Much	=	Quanto

A

A: un/uno/una
About To: in procinto di
Against: contro
Although: sebbene
And: e
As…As: così… come
At (place): a
At What Time: a che ora
A Little: un po'
Above: sopra
Ago: fa
Already: già
And Now, What: e adesso cosa
As Long As: fintanto che
At (hour): alle
Awful: terribile
A Little Bit: un po'
After: dopo
All: tutto
Also: anche
Another: un altro

As Soon As: non appena
At this Moment: in questo momento
A Lot: molto/tanto
Afterwards: in seguito
All Day: tutto il giorno
Always: sempre
Anybody: chiunque
About: circa
Again: di nuovo
Almost: quasi
Amusing: divertente
As: come
Appointed: designato
At This Time: a quest'ora

B

Barely: appena
Between: tra
Butter: burro
Because: perché
Bit: po'

By: di
Before: prima
Both: tutti e due
By The Way: a proposito
Behind: dietro
Breakdown: esaurimento
Below: sotto
But: ma

C

Careful: attento
Caution: attenzione
Certain: sicuro

D

Dear: caro
Difficult: difficile
Departure: partenza
Despite: nonostante

Detour: deviazione
Divided By: diviso da

F

Fair: giusto
Fine: bene
Further: ulteriore
Far: lontano
For: per
Fault: colpa
For The Reason: per questa ragione
Feasible: fattibile
Few: pochi
From: da

G

Generally: generalmente
Good: buono

H

Half: metà

How Long: per quanto
Heavy: pesante
How Much: quanto
How: come
Hot: caldo

I

If: se
Impossible: impossibile
In front of: di fronte a
In good health: in buona salute
Inside: dentro
It is necessary: se necessario
Immediately: immediatamente
Improbable: improbabile
In case of: in caso di
In order that: in modo che
Instead of: invece di
It could be: potrebbe essere
In: in/a

In case that: nel caso in cui
In order to: in modo da
In spite of: nonostante
It maybe: può essere
Important: importante
In a hurry: di fretta
Included: incluso
In the habit of: con l'abitudine di
Interesting:

J

Just: solo/appena

K

Keep: mantenere
Kind: tipo (*noun*)/gentile (*adj.*)

L

Lacking: mancante
Latest: ultimo
Least: meno

Likely: probabilmente
List: elenco
Low: basso
Large: grande/ampio
Left: sinistra
Little: piccolo
Last: ultimo
Leftover: avanzo
Long: lungo
Late: tardi
Looks Like: sembra
Later: più tardi
Less: meno

M
Made In: fatto in
Mrs.: Sig.ra
Many: molti
Much: molto

Maybe: forse
Merely: semplicemente
Miss.: Sig.na
More: più

N
Named (to be): (essere) chiamato
Neither: nessuno dei due
Nothing: niente
Narrow: stretto
Never: mai
Now: ora
Near: vicino
New: nuovo
Nearby: nelle vicinanze
Next: successivo
Necessary: necessario
Next to: vicino a
Not: non

O
Obvious: ovvio
On: sopra/su
Open: aperto
Outside: fuori
Odd: dispari/bizzarro
On Call: in chiamata
Or: oppure/o
Over: al di sopra di
Of: di
Once: una volta
Other: altro
Overcome: superare
Of course: di certo
Ongoing: in corso
Otherwise: altrimenti
Overlook: trascurare
Often: spesso

Only: solo
Out: fuori

P
Percent: percento
Point: punto
Push: spingere
Perhaps: forse
Probable: probabile
Pleasant: piacevole
Problem: problema
Perfectly: perfettamente
Program: programma
Please: per favore
Pull: tirare

Q
Question: domanda
Quite Enough: abbastanza
R
Ready: pronto

Repeat: ripetere
Routine: routine
Regularly: regolarmente
Right Away: subito
Responsible: responsabile
Right Now: proprio ora
Ridiculous: ridicolo
Relative: parente(*noun*)/relativo(*adj*)

S
See you Later: a dopo
Sir: Sig.
Something: qualcosa
Still: ancora(*adv*)/fermo(*adj*)
Several: parecchi
So: così
Somewhat: piuttosto
Stop: fermare
Show Me: Fammi vedere
Some: alcuni
So Much: davvero tanto

Subject: soggetto
Side: lato
Somebody: qualcuno
Soon: presto
Sure: sicuro
Similar: simile
Someone:qualcuno
Specific: specifico
Somewhere: da qualche parte

T
Task: compito
The: il/lo/la/i/gli/le
Together: insieme
Too (also): anche
There Will Be: ci sarà
That: che/quello
There: là
Through: attraverso
Those: quelli
Therefore: perciò

These: questi
To: a
Too Much: troppo/troppi
There is/are: c'è/ci sono
Thick: spesso
Tomorrow: domani
This Evening: questa sera
There Have Been: ci sono stati
This: questo
Thing: cosa
Tonight: stanotte
There was/were: c'era/c'erano
There Would Be: ci sarebbero

U
Underneath: sotto
Unlikely: improbabile
Unwilling: riluttante
Under: sotto
Up: su
Until: fino

Useful: utile
Understood: capito
Unless: salvo che
Unfortunately: sfortunatamente
Unpleasant: spiacevole

V
Very: molto

W
Warm: caldo
Why: perché
Where To: dove
With: con
Whatever: qualunque cosa
Whereby: per cui
Whoever: chiunque
Watch Out: attento
Wide: ampio
With Me: con me
Whether: se

Well: bene
Which: quale
With you: con te
Whole: intero
Whereabouts: in che luogo
Wet Paint: vernice fresca
What: cosa
When: quando
Where: dove
Whenever: ogni volta
Within: entro
While: mentre
Who: chi
Without: senza
Whose: di chi

Y
Yet: ancora
Yield: rendimento (noun)

Learning Step 5

Reflexives, Direct Object, Indirect Object Pronouns and Possessives Adjective

are essential to complete a sentence

Practice them, emphasize the pronunciation

Lesson 3: Part 3

Direct Object / Diretti

Italian/English/Spelling   Examples

Mi	(Meh)	(Me)	Call me	Chiamami
Ti	(Tee)	(You)	Bring you	Ti porto
Lo	(Loh)	(Him)	Take him	Portalo
La	(Lah)	(Her)	Invite her	Invitala
Ci	(Chi)	(Us)	Get us	Prendici
Vi	(Vee)	(You)	Buy for you	Comprarvi
Li	(Lee)	(Them)	Call them	Chiamali
Lo	(Loh)	(It)	Sell it	Vendilo

You	have	to go	to take him home
(Tu)	lo devi	andare	a portare a casa
(Voi)	dovete	andare	a portarla a casa
He	can	come	to see me later
(Lui)	può	venire	a trovarmi dopo
(Lui)	mi può	venire	a trovare dopo
They	want	to bring	her to see you
(Loro)	vogliono	portarla	a trovarti
They	are	trying	to call him today
(Essi)	stanno	provando	a chiamarlo oggi

Indirective Object / Indiretto

Examples   Italian/English/Spelling

Sent me	Mi ha mandato	Mi	(Mee)	(to/for)me
Speak to you	Parlarti	Ti	(Tee)	(to/for)you
Tell him	Digli	Gli	(Glee)	(to/for)him
Explain to her	Spiegale	Le	(Leh)	(to/for)her
Taught us	Ci insegnò	Ci	(Chi)	(to/for)us
Advise you	Consigliarvi	Vi	(Vee)	(to/for)you
Say to them	Dire loro	Gli/loro	(Glee)	(to/for)them
Give to it	Dargli	Gli	(Glee)	(to/for)it

Mr Brambilla		taught us		Italian
Il signor Brambilla		ci ha insegnato		l'italiano
What		are you saying		to them?
Cosa		dic		loro?
Lucia,	your father	wants		to speak to you!
Lucia,	tuo padre	vuole		parlarti
I		want	to phone him	
(Io)		voglio	chiamarlo	
Someone	sent me		a postcard	from Spain
Qualcuno	mi ha mandato	una cartolina		dalla Spagna

Reflexive Pronoun/ Pron. riflessivi

Italian/English/Spelling   Examples

Mi	(Meh)	Myself	I wash myself	Mi lavo
Ti	(Tee)	Yourself	You dress yourself	Ti vesti
Si	(See)	Himself	He woke up	Si svegliò
Si	(See)	Herself	She dress herself	Si veste
Ci	(Chi)	Ourselves	We wash ourselves	Ci laviamo
Vi	(Vee)	Yourselves	Brush yourselves	Vi pettinate
Si	(See)	Themselves	Wash themselves	Si lavano
Si	(See)	Itself	It wash itself	si lava

Possessive Adjectives/Agg. possessivi

Examples   Italian/English/Spelling

My home	La mia casa	Mio/a	(Mee-oh)	My
Your car	La tua auto	Tuo/a	(Too-oh)	Your
His son	Suo figlio	Suo/a	(Soo-oh)	His
Her pet	Il suo animale	Suo/a	(Soo-oh)	Her
Our boat	La nostra barca	Nostro/a	(Nohs-troh)	Our
Your dad	Vostro padre	Vostro/a	(Vohstroh)	Your
Their idea	La loro idea	Loro	(Lohroh)	Their
Its tail	La sua coda	Suo/a	(Soo-oh)	Its

I	want	to get up		
(Io)	voglio	alzarmi		
(Io)	mi voglio	alzare		
I	look	at myself	in the	mirror
(Io)	mi guardo		allo	specchio
(Io)	guardo	me	allo	specchio
I	prepare	the dinner for myself		
(Io)	mi preparo	la cena		
We	kissed	each other		
(Noi)	ci siamo baciati			

You	are	welcome to	our house	
(Voi)	siete	benvenuti a	casa nostra	
She	is	driving	my	car
(Lei)	sta	guidando	la mia	auto
He	has	to bring	my	son
(Lui)	deve	portare	mio	figlio
They	want	to take	my	wife
(Loro)	vogliono	prendere	mia	moglie
Today	I want	to go	to my	studio
Oggi	voglio	andare	al mio	ufficio

Notes on Reflexives : In Italian a direct and indirect object pronoun can also be placed right after the noun (at the very beginning of the phrase).

Examples :

I will bring them home
Li porterò a casa
Porterò **loro** a casa

I want to take him to the airport
Lo voglio portare a casa
Voglio portar**lo** a casa

I have to go to purchase the medicines for him
Gli devo andare a comprare le medicine
Devo andare a comprar**gli** le medicine

I can prepare the food for you at twelve
Ti posso preparare da mangiare a mezzogiorno
Posso preparar**ti** da mangiare a mezzogiorno

Learning Step 6

The Infinitive Verbs

Are the foundation of this course they are used almost identically both in English and Italian

Practice them!

Lesson 4: Part 1

What is an Infinitive Verb?

1) Well, it starts with a "To" in English and ends with "**ARE/ERE/IRE**" in Italian

    Example: <u>to</u> call   <u>to</u> be   <u>to</u> come   <u>to</u> eat

            chiam<u>are</u>   ess<u>ere</u>   veni<u>re</u>   mangi<u>are</u>

2) It's never the 1st. verb (as it can't be conjugated)

| You can't say in English | I to call | I to be | I to come | I to eat |
| You can't say in Italian | Io chiamare | Io essere | Io venire | Io mangiare |

3) But it's always used after the 2nd. Infinitive Verb.

    Example: I   want   to go   to eat

           Io   voglio   andare   a mangiare

           She wants   to come   to visit us

           Lei vuole   venire   a trovarci

This course is built around the Infinitive Verbs

In English, infinitive verbs are used all the time:
I want to go to eat now.
He wants to come to visit you.

Italian use The Infinitive Verbs the same way

All the time and in the same way we do !

I	want	to go	to eat	now
(Io)	voglio	andare	a mangiare	ora
He	wants	to come	to visit you	
(Lui)	vuole	venire	a trovarti	

SMILE ☺ Both sentences mirror each other, except for the Italian vowel "a" (ah) which is added in front of the 2nd infinitive verb .

This course is built around <u>the Infinitive Verbs</u>

Here are more examples!

I	have	to take	you	She	wants	to watch TV	'til midnight
Io	devo	prendere	te	Lei	vuole	guardare la TV	fino a mezzanotte
You	have	to bring	him	We	want	to go to shop	at noon
Tu	devi	prendere	lui	Noi	vogliamo	andare a comprare	a mezzogiorno
He	has	to go to see	you	They	want	to give you	a surprise
Lui	deve	andare a trovare	te	Loro	vogliono	darti	una sorpresa
We	have	to try to get	there	You	want	to do him	a lot of good
Noi	dobbiamo	cercare di arrivare	là	Tu	vuoi	fargli	un sacco di bene

All You Need To Be Conversant in Italian are "The Infinitive Verbs"
which are the Foundation of this method.

- The Infinitive Verbs are used the same way and even on the same spot in both Italian and English .

- The Infinitive Verbs are never the 1st.Verb on a phrase :

I want to have
Voglio avere

- The Infinitive Verbs start with "To" in English:
And End with ARE/ERE/IRE in Italian:

To have
Avere

- The Infinitive Verbs cannot be conjugated: I to have
Io avere

- The Infinitive Verbs continue to be used on a phrase endlessly.
In this sense the 2 languages are identical

I want to go to eat
Voglio andare a mangiare

- The 2nd. Infinitive Verb on a Italian Phrase
is always Preceded by an "A"

I want to go to sleep
Voglio andare a dormire

The infinitive Verbs enable through templates to be conversant in four tenses:
(1) Gerund-action, (2) Past Participle, (3) Future and (4) Conditional.

On the Next Page
You'll Find A
List Of,

__Verbi Infiniti__
Infinitive Verbs

Study, Read and Spell them multiple times 'till they stick and...... Notice that all of them (well almost all)

Start with __To__ in English
End with ARE/ERE/IRE in Italian

A

To Accept: accettare
To Acquire: acquisire
To Allow: permettere
To Announce: annunciare
To Answer: rispondere
To Argue: discutere
To Approve: approvare
To Arrive: arrivare
To Arrange: organizzare
To Ask: chiedere
To Assist: assistere

B

To Be: essere
To Be Angry: essere arrabbiato
To Be Right: avere ragione
To Be Thankful: essere grati
To Be Wrong: avere torto
To Become: diventare
To Begin: iniziare
To Believe: credere
To Bring: portare
To Build: costruire
To Buy: comprare

C

To Cause: causare
To Call: chiamare
Can: potere
To Clean: pulire
To Close: chiudere
To Collect: raccogliere
To Come: venire
To Complete: completare
To Cook: cucinare
To Copy: copiare
To Correct: correggere
Could: potrebbe
To Cry: piangere

D

To Dance: ballare
To Depart: partire
To Discuss: discutere
To Do: fare
To Doubt: dubitare
To Dress: vestire
To Drink: bere
To Drive: guidare

E

To Earn: guadagnare
To Eat: mangiare
To Enter: entrare
To Erase: cancellare
To Exit: uscire

F

To Fall: cadere
To Fear: temere
To Feel: sentire
To Find: trovare
To Find Out: scorprire
To Finish: finire
To Fit: adattarsi
To Follow: seguire
To Forget: dimenticare
To Forgive: perdonare

G

To Get: ottenere
To Give: dare
To Go: andare
To Greet: salutare
To Grow: crescere

L

To Laugh: ridere
To Learn: imparare
To Leave: lasciare
To Lend: prestare
To Listen: ascoltare
To Let; lasciare
To Like: piacere
To Live: vivere
To Look: guardare
To Look (like): somigliare
To Lose: perdere
To Love: amare
To Live: vivere

M

May: potere
To Make: fare
To Move: muovere
Must: dovere

N

To Name: nominare
To Need: avere bisogno
To Nix: negare, proibire (slang)

O

To Obey: obbedire
To Offer: offrire
To Observe: osservare
To Open: aprire
To Order: ordinare
To Owe: dovere, essere in debito
To Own: possedere

P

To Pardon: perdonare
To Pay: pagare
To Pick(select): scegliere
To Pick: prendere
To Play (instrument): suonare
To Pull: tirare
To Purchase: acquistare
To Push: spingere
To Put: mettere

R

To Read: leggere
To Realize: realizzare
To Refuse: rifiutare
To Reject: rifiutare/respingere
To Remember: ricordare
To Repeat: ripetere
To Reply: rispondere
To Request: richiedere
To Respect: rispettare
To Rest: riposare
To Return: ritornare
To Run: correre

S

To Save: salvare/risparmiare
To Satisfy: soddisfare
To Say: dire
To See: vedere
To Seek: cercare
To Sell: vendere
To Send: mandare
Shall: dovere
Should: dovrebbe
To Show: mostrare
To Shop: comprare
To Sit: sedere

To Sleep: dormire
To Smile: sorridere
To Solve: risolvere
To Speak: parlare
To Start: iniziare
To Study: studiare

T

To Take: prendere
To Take (keep): tenere
To Talk: parlare
To Teach: insegnare
To Tell: dire
To Terminate: finire
To Thank: ringrziare
To Think: pensare
To Travel: viaggiare
To Trot: trottare
To Try: cercare

U

To Understand : capire
To Use: usare
To Utilize: utilizzare

V

To Value; valutare/apprezzare

To Visit: visitare

W

To Wait: aspettare
To Walk: camminare
To Want: volere
To Wash: lavare
To Watch: guardare
To Wear: indossare
To Wish: desiderare
To Win: vincere
To Work: lavorare/funzionare
To Write: scrivere

Y

To Yawn: sbadigliare

Z

To Zip: comprimere

Learning Step 7

The '4' Trigger verbs

enable you to initiate any basic conversation

Practice them, especially the conjugations and the pronunciation

The following 4 "Trigger Verbs"

Enable you to initiate most conversations

Lesson No. 5	**Lesson No. 6**
<u>To be</u> Essere	<u>To have</u> Avere
Lesson No. 7	**Lesson No. 8**
<u>To want</u> Volere	<u>Can</u> Potere

The 1st. Trigger Verb is "To Be"

Let us first review the Verb "ESSERE" (Eh-sseh-reh) :

Examples of ESSERE

		I	**am**	**tall**	**He**	**is**	**a**	**policeman**
Io	sono (sonoh)	Io	sono	alto	Lui	è		un poliziotto
Tu	sei (she-ee)	**She**	**is**	**smart**	**You**	**are**		**single**
Lui	è (Ehs)	Lei	è	intelligente	Voi	siete		single
Lei	è (Ehs)	**They**	**are**	**fanatics**	**He**	**is**		**late**
Noi	siamo(seeah-moh)	Loro		sono	fanatici	Lui	è	in ritardo
Voi	siete (see-eh-teh)	**It**	**is**	**late**	**She**	**is**		**beautiful**
Essi	sono (soh-noh)		è	tardi	Lei	è		bella

The Trigger Verbs: **To be = Essere**

I am a good player Sono un buon giocatore	**You are never on time** Non sei mai puntuale
I am a great person Sono un'ottima persona	**They are the best in town** Sono i migliori in città
You are a good man Sei una brava persona	**They are the worst there is** Sono il peggio ci sia
You are a disgusting person Sei una persona disgustosa	**It is better if you don't come** È meglio se non vieni
He is an excellent student È uno studente eccellente	**You are tired every day** Sei sempre stanco
He is a fantastic cook È un cuoco fantastico	**You are upset about the game** Sei arrabbiato per la partita
We are always here for you Siamo sempre qui per te	**You are frustrated by the whole situation** Siete frustrati da tutta la situazione
We are the same people Siamo le stesse persona	**They are very tired after the trip** Sono davvero stanchi dopo il viaggio
You are a winning team Siamo un team vincente	

The 2nd Trigger Verb is "To Have"

Let us review first the Verb "AVERE" in Italian.

Examples using Avere (Ah-veh-reh)

I	Io	**ho (oh)**	
You	Tu	**hai** (ahi)	
c.			
He	Lui	**ha** (ah)	
She	Lei	**ha** (ah)	
We	Noi	**abbiamo (ahbee-ah-moh)**	
You	Voi	**avete (ah-veh-teh).**	
They	Essi	**hanno (ah-noh)**	
It		**ha** (ah)	

I have gotten mail today
Io ho   ricevuto l'email oggi

You   have taken a long time
Ci   hai messo un sacco di tempo

She has slept in the morning
Lei. ha   dormito durante la mattina

They   have studied all day
Loro hanno studiato tutto il giorno

They have cooked all morning
Loro hanno cucinato tutta la mattina

He has been running all afternoon
Lui ha corso tutto il pomeriggio

I   have a dog
Io   ho   un cane

You   have not called me
Tu   non mi hai chiamato

He   has   done his work
Lui   ha   fatto il suo lavoro

She   has   taken me   home
Lei   mi ha   portata   a casa

I   have not did it
Io   non l'ho fatto

They have not watched TV
Loro non hanno guardato la TV

Lesson 6: Part 2

Here are examples of the Verb "Haber" (ahvehreh) in Italian, It is used as an auxiliary verb to speak in Past Participle

To Have: Avere

I have done	**They have studied**	**You have understood**
Ho fatto	Hanno studiato	Hai capito
I have gotten	**I have run**	**He has written**
Ho ottenuto	Ho corso	Ha scritto
I have taken	**She has walked**	**You have improved**
Ho preso	Ha camminato	Hai migliorato
You have cooked	**They have called**	**They have thought**
Hai cucinato	Hanno chiamato	Hanno pensato
He has waited	**I have spoken**	**You have brought it**
Ha aspettato	Ho parlato	L'hai comprato
She has seen	**I have bought it**	**She has washed**
Ha visto	L'ho comprato	Ha lavato

Avere	Dovere	Participio passato
I have a great family	**I have to see you tomorrow**	**I have received mail today**
Ho una famiglia fantastica	Devo vederlo domani	Ho ricevuto una lettera offi
I have a headache	**I have to come to see you**	**I have slept well yesterday night**
Ho male alla testa	Devo venire a vederti	Ho dormito bene la scorsa notte
You have four good kids	**You have to go to eat**	**Yo have not done your work**
Avete quattro bravi ragazzi	Devi andare a mangiare	Non hai fatto il tuo lavoro
I have a good job	**I have to meet with him today**	**I have seen her early today**
Ho un buon lavoro	Devo incontrarmi con lui oggi	L'ho vista stamattina presto
He has problems with her	**He has to bring him the food**	**He has made a big mistake**
Ha problemi con lei	Deve portargli del cibo	Ha commesso un grande errore
They have a great life	**They have to hurry up**	**They have eaten a lot today**
Hanno una bella vita	Devono affrettarsi	Hanno mangiato molto oggi
You have a lot of luck	**You have to finish the project**	**We have sent her to school**
Hai molta fortuna	Devi finire il progetto	L'abbiamo mandata a scuola
I have a rough road ahead	**We have to start moving**	**You have been absent lately**
Ho un cammino difficile davanti a me	Dobbiamo iniziare a muoverci	Siete stati assenti ultimamente
You have a lot of luck	**She has to pay attention**	**She has bought new clothes**
Avete molta fortuna	Debe fare attenzione	Ha comprato vestiti nuovi
She has a brand new car	**It has to be fixed**	**It has been repaired already**
Ha un'auto nuova	Deve essere aggiustato	E' già stato aggiustato
It has a broken light	**I have to start all over again**	**I have been thinking about it**
Ha una luce rotta	Devo ricominciare tutto di nuovo	Ho pensato a te

**3rd . Trigger Verb "To Want" is used in Italian
to Express either Desire or To Give an order:**

Let us now review the Verb "VOLERE" (?) in Italian, it has two forms:
  1) The Verb "Volere" in Italian is used to express a desire or a wish
  2) The Verb "Volere che" is used to express a command, request or order.

To Want   **Examples**

Volere (Voh-leh-reh)	**To express a desire**	**To give an order**
I Io voglio **(Voh-glee-oh)**	**I want to go to sleep**	**I want you to go to eat**
You Tu vuoi **(Voo-oh-ee)**	Voglio andare a dormire	Voglio che tu vada a mangiare
He Lui vuole **(Voo-oh-leh)**	**I want to learn Italian**	**He wants you to write to him**
She Lei vuole **(Voo-oh-leh)**	Voglio imparare l'italiano	Vuole che gli scrivi
We Noi vogliamo **(Noh-ee)**	**She wants to cook for you**	**We want you to think about it**
You Voi volete **(Voh-leh-teh)**	Vuole cucinare per te	Vogliamo che ci pensi tu
They Loro vogliono **(Vohgleeohnoh)**	**They want to take you home**	**I want you to bring me the check**
It (Esso) vuole **(Voo-oh-leh)**	Vogliono portarti a casa	Voglio che mi porti il conto

Volere		Volere che
Desire / Wish Desiderare/Volere	<u>Examples</u>	<u>**Command / Order**</u> Comando/Ordine
I want to take you to the movies Voglio portarti al cinema		**I want that you stop calling me** Voglio che la smetti di chiamarmi
I want to go shopping today after lunch Voglio andare a fare shipping dopo pranzo		**I want that you think about it carefully** Voglio che ci pensi attentamente
You want me to bring you anything? Vuoi che ti porti qualcosa?		**Do you want that we get him ready?** Vuoi che lo prepariamo?
He wants to buy a brand new pair of shoes Vuole comprare un paio di scarpe nuovo		**He wants that you call him today at 2 p.m.** Vuole che lo chiami alle 14:00
She wants to try to find a new job Vuole cercare di trovare un nuovo lavoro		**She wants me not to bother her anymore** Non vuole che le dia più fastidio

**The 4th Trigger Verb "Can" is used in Italian to express "Being Able To"
In Italian means "Potere" (Pohtehreh)**

Poder (Pohtehreh)	Examples:	Examples:
Io posso (Poh-soh)	**I can see you later**	**He can come at noon**
Tu puoi (Poo-oh-ee)	Posso vederti dopo	Può venire a mezzogiorno
Lui può (poo-oh)	**She can go to see him**	**You can do it**
Lei può (poo-oh)	Può andare a vederlo	Puoi farlo
Noi possiamo (poh-see-ah-moh)	**They can take you home**	**You can come in**
Voi potete (poh-teh-teh))	Possono portarti a casa	Puoi entrare
Loro possono (poh-soh-noh)	**He can come tomorrow**	**I can call you later**
	Può venire domani	Posso chiamarti dopo

Examples of verb Potere

I can come to see you this weekend
Posso venire a vederti questo fine settimana

I can call you every night at 8 p.m.
Posso chiamarti tutte le sere alle 20:00.

He can take them to the park tomorrow at 4
Può portarli al parco domani alle 16:00

She can not eat chicken
Lei non può mangiare pollo

We can work together to solve the problem
Possiamo lavorare insieme per risolvere il problema

He can prepare for the test this week
Può prepararsi sul test questa settimana

You can bring them over to spend the day here
Puoi portarli a passare il giorno qui

You can go to the movies with them
Potete andare al cinama con lei

You can call me after lunch
Puoi chiamarmi dopo pranzo

They can complain all they want, it won't make a difference
Possono lamentarsi quanto vogliono, non farà differenza

Ok. Let's use the Nouns, The 4 Trigger Verbs, The Magic Words and additional Infinitive Verbs to build more phrases.

I   Io
You Tu
He   Lui
She Lei
We Noi
You Voi
They Loro

The 4 Trigger Verbs

To Be   Essere (Eh-seh-reh)

To Have Avere (Ah-veh-reh)

To Want Volere (Voh-leh-reh)

Can   Potere (Poh-Teh-Reh)

I have to go to call her
Devo andare a chiamarla

I want to take you to dinner
Voglio portarti a cena

He can wait for you at noon
Può aspettarti a mezzogiorno

I have to go to take notes
Devo andare a prendere note

I can go to see you tomorrow
Posso venire a trovarti domani

We can cook rather quickly
Possiamo cucinare abbastanza rapidamente

We have to wait for her
Dobbiamo aspettarla

I want to come to see you
Voglio venire a trovarti

You can go to sleep
Puoi andare a dormire

She wants to cook for you
Lei vuole cucinare per te

I have to run to go to see him
Devo correre per andare a vederlo

They can come to run tonight
Possono venire a correre stanotte

He has to call her soon
Deve chiamarla presto

Additional Trigger Verbs:

Examples

To Go	**Andare** (andare)	
To Come	**Venire** (veh-nee-reh)	
To Take	**Prendere** (prendere)	
To Buy	**Comprare** (comprare)	
To Cook	**Cucinare** (Koocheenare)	
To Wait	**Aspettare** (aspetare)	
To Run	**Correre** (correre)	
To Watch	**Guardare** (gooardare)	
To See	**Vedere** (vedere)	
To Give	**Dare** (Dahreh)	
To Get	**Ricevere** (richevere)	
To Get	**Ottenere** (otenere)	
To Walk	**Camminare** (caminare)	
To Write	**Scrivere** (scrivere)	
To Read	**Leggere** (Leyere)	

You have to come to see her
Dovete venire a vederla

You can come to watch TV later
Puoi venire a vedere la Tv dopo

She wants you to call soon
Vuole che la chiami presto

He can read pretty well
Lui può leggere piuttosto bene

They have to run today
Devono correre oggi

She wants to run every morning
Lei vuole correre ogni mattina

They can take you to the airport now
Loro possono portarti all'aeroporto ora

You can go to buy groceries at three
Puoi andare a fare la spesa alle tre

He has to get mail this week
Deve ricevere posta questa settimana

He has to go to get his ID
Deve andare a prendere il suo ID

He has to learn to write often
Deve imparare a scrivere spesso

Lesson 9: Part 3

Now, "Let's" build phrases with what we have learned

I have to be a good father
Devo essere un buon padre

I want to be fair
Voglio essere giusto

I can be often late
Posso essere spesso in ritardo

You have to be persistent
Devi essere persistente

You want to be the best
Vuoi essere il migliore

You can be the last to come in
Puoi essere l'ultimo ad entrare

We have to be polite
Dobbiamo essere educati

We want to be the best
Vogliamo essere i migliori

I have to be there on time
Devo essere là in tempo

I want to be present
Voglio essere presente

I can be there at two
Posso essere lì alle due

You have to be alert all the time
Devi essere sempre attento

You want to be ahead of the curve
Vuoi essere davanti alla curva

You can have a lot of trouble soon
Puoi avere molti problemi presto

We have to be waiting for him at the gate
Dobbiamo aspettarlo al cancello

He can be available later
Può essere disponibile più tardi

He has to be patient
Deve essere paziente

He wants to be like his father
Vuole essere come suo padre

He can be a very good team mate
Può essere un buonissimo compagno di squadra

We want to be ready for him
Vogliamo essere pronti per lui

We can be in the losing end
Possiamo essere dal lato dei perdenti

He has to be devastated
Dev'essere devastato

He wants to be permanently on vacations
Vuole essere sempre in vacanza

We can be of great help to you
Possiamo esserti di grande aiuto

The Infinitive Verbs/ The Four Trigger Verbs

Ininitive Verbs		To Be	To Want	To Have	Can
Nouns		Essere	Volere	Avere	Potere
I	Io	Sono	Voglio	Ho	Posso
You	Tu	Sei	Vuoi	Hai	Puoi
He	Lui	É	Vuole	Ha	Può
She	Lei	É	Vuole	Ha	Può
We	Noi	Siamo	Vogliamo	Abbiamo	Possiamo
You	Voi	Siete	Volete	Avete	Potete
They	Loro	Sono	Vogliono	Hanno	Possono
It		É	Vuole	Ha	Può

Learning Step 8

The 4 Templates

Enable you to be conversant in:

- Gerund (action),

- Past Participle,

- Future

and

- Conditional tenses ,

while using only "Infinitive Verbs"

ENGLISH: To be + Verb ending in **"ing"**

ITALIAN: Stare (to stay) + Verbo che termina in **"ando"** o **"endo"**

Io sto
Tu stai
Egli sta
Noi stiamo
Voi state
Essi stanno

How to convert an:

- English "Infinitive Verb" into Gerund

To Go—Kill "To"—add "ing" = *Going*

- Italian "Infinitive Verb" into Gerundio

Andare---Kill "ARE"—add "ando"= *Andando*

Example: To Go=Andare (Infinitive verb)

I am going to eat

Sto andando a mangiare

Gerund

<u>English</u> : To Be + Verb ending in **"ing"**
<u>Italian</u> : Stare (To Stay) + Verb ending in **"ando"** e **"endo"**

- In English we speak in Gerund when we refer to <u>"Action."</u>
- And we use the Verb <u>"To Be"</u> followed by a verb ending in <u>ing.</u>
- In Italian the same, but they use the verb <u>"To Stay"</u>

<u>Example:</u>
To Call: I am   go*ing*   to eat
                 Io sto   and*ando*   a mangiare

So, bottom line: verb endings in <u>ing</u> in English end in either **ando** or **endo** in Italian

<u>How to convert an Infinitive Verb to Gerund:</u>
<u>In English</u> we do this:
To Call----Calling (kill the <u>"To"</u> add <u>"ing"</u>)
<u>In Italian</u> they do this:
Chiamare---- Chiamando (kill <u>"are"</u> add <u>"ando"</u>)

Examples:

Gerund (action)

I am calling you now	**They are calling him today**	**They are calling tonight**
Ti sto chiamando ora	Lo stanno chiamando oggi	Stanno chiamando stanotte
I am studying all morning	**They are studying today**	**She is studying now**
Sto studiando da tutta la mattina	Oggi stanno studiando	Sta studiando adesso
I am waiting at the house	**We are waiting for you**	**You are waiting in vain**
Sto aspettando in casa	Loro vi stanno aspettando	Stai aspettando invano
I am writing to you every week	**They are writing every other week**	**He is writing often**
Ti sto scrivendo ogni settimana	Loro stanno scrivendo ogni due settimane	Lui sta scrivendo spesso
I am trying to visit you	**She is trying to visit us**	**They are trying to call**
Sto cercando di visitarti	Sta cercando di visitarci	Stanno cercando di chiamare
I am learning to speak Italian	**She is learning about the country**	**He is learning the basic**
Sto imparando a parlare italiano	Sta imparando sul paese	Lei sta imparando le basi
I am watching italian TV	**You are watching her grow**	**He is watching the game**
Sto guardando la TV italiana	Voi la state guardando crescere	Lui sta guardando la partita

Infinitive Verbs:

To Call : Chiamare   To Study: Studiare   To Wait: Aspettare   To Write: Scrivere   To Try: Cercare

To Learn: Imparare   To Watch: Guardare

2. Participle/Participio

How to Convert an "Infinitive Verb" in Italian into a past **Participle Verb**:

Regular Past Participles are formed by dropping the infinitive endings -are, -ere, or -ire and adding, respectively, the suffixes **-ato**, **-uto**, or **-ito**.

Camminare (to walk):   *camminato* (walked)
Credere (to believe):   *creduto* (believed)
Capire (to understand):   *capito* (understood)

Past participles are part of every Italian **COMPOUND TENSE**, together with a conjugation of the auxiliary verb *Essere* (To be) or *Avere* (To have).
Transitive verbs (with direct objects) mostly take *Avere* as auxiliary verb; verbs of movement, reflexive and reciprocal verbs, and some other intransitive verbs use *Essere*.

Example:

To Wait= Aspettare (Infinitive verb)
I have waited for you
Ti ho *aspettato*

To Go= Andare (Infinitive verb)
She has gone to school
Lei è *andata* a scuola

English: To have = In Italian: Avere   Examples in Past participle:

To be = In Italian: Essere

To take: I have taken her home	**To wait: They have waited for you**
Portare : L'ho portata a casa	Aspettare: Loro vi hanno aspettati
To eat: He has eaten at 12	**To wash: She has been washing all morning**
Mangiare: Ha mangiato alle 12	Lavare: Lei ha lavato tutta la mattina
To learn: They have learned to read	**To ask: He has been asking for you**
Imparare: Hanno imparato a leggere	Chiedere: Lui ha chiesto di voi
To talk: She has talked to him	**To cook: They have been cooking today**
Parlare: Lei ha parlato con lui	Cucinare: Loro hanno cucinato oggi
To study: We have studied	**To walk: We have walked**
Studiare: Abbiamo studiato	Camminare: Noi abbiamo camminato
To get: They have gotten no email	**To think: You have thought about it**
Ricevere: Non han ricevuto nessuna email	Pensare: Tu lo hai pensato
To go: I have gone to see her	**To come: You have been coming every year**
Andare: Sono andato a vederla	Venire: Voi siete venuti ogni anno
To bring: He has brought a friend	**To win: We have been winning more**
Portare: Ha portato un amico	Vincere: Noi abbiamo vinto di più
To listen: She has listened to him	**To buy: I have been buying lots of vitamins**
Ascolare: Lei lo ha ascoltato	Comprare: Ho comprato un sacco di vitamine

For a list of Past Participle Verbs see Next Page.

Past Participle (Verbs)/(Verbi) Participio passato

Been *Stato*	**Had** *Avuto*	**Arrived** *Arrivato*	**Washed** *Lavato*	**Cooled** *Raffreddato*	**Packed** *Confezionato*	**Written** *Scritto*	**Fought** *Combattuto*
Come *Venuto*	**Talked** *Parlato*	**Calculated** *Calcolato*	**Explained** *Spiegato*	**Looked** *Guardato*	**Brought** *Portato*	**Replied** *Risposto*	**Thought** *Pensado*
Gotten *Ricevuto*	**Taken** *Preso*	**Seen** *Visto*	**Repeated** *Ripetuto*	**Appealed** *Appellato*	**Needed** *Necessitato*	**Heated** *Scaldato*	**Watched** *Guardato*
Ran *Corso*	**Cleaned** *Pulito*	**Called** *Chiamato*	**Born** *Nato*	**Finished** *Finito*	**Disputed** *Contestato*	**Cooked** *Cucinato*	**Replied** *Risposto*
Done *Fatto*	**Failed** *Mancato*	**Given** *Dato*	**Listened** *Ascoltatao*	**Accepted** *Accettati*	**Built** *Costruito*	**Traveled** *Viaggiato*	**Grabbed** *Afferrato*
Wished *Desiderato*	**Made** *Fatto*	**Walked** *Camminato*	**Bought** *Comprato*	**Asked** *Chiesto*	**Wanted** *Voluto*	**Realized** *Realizzato*	**Started** *Iniziato*
Remembered *Ricordato*	**Baked** *Infornato*	**Put** *Messo*	**Sat** *Seduto*	**Read** *Letto*	**Eaten** *Mangiato*	**Gone** *Andato*	**Enjoyed** *Goduto*
Fried *Fritto*	**Heard** *Sentito*	**Lost** *Perso*	**Liked** *Piaciuto*	**Washed** *Lavato*	**Bathed** *Bagnato*	**Said** *Detto*	**Searched** *Cercato*
Slept *Dormito*	**Agreed** *Concordato*	**Exited** *Uscito*	**Left** *Lasciato*	**Loved** *Amato*	**Woken** *Svegliato*	**Layed** *Deposto*	**Saddened** *Rattristito*
Questioned *Interrogato*	**Entered** *Inserito*	**Hurt** *Ferito*	**Found** *Trovato*	**Flown** *Volato*	**Won** *Vinto*	**Cried** *Pianto*	**Shipped** *nviato*
Ordered *Ordinato*	**Boiled** *Bollito*	**Dreamed** *Sognato*	**Drank** *Bevuto*	**Paid** *Pagato*	**Swam** *Nuotato*	**Waited** *Aspettato*	**Started** *Iniziato*
Answered *Risposto*	**Understood** *Capito*	**Argued** *Discusso*	**Jumped** *Saltato*	**Forgotten** *Dimenticato*	**Arrived** *Arrivato*	**Dried** *Asciugato*	**Shown** *Mostrato*

The **future simple** tense is used to talk about an <u>action which has yet to happen</u>
To form the future of Italian regular verbs it is necessary **to kill ARE/ERE/IRE** and **add the correct endings** to the root of the verb.

Example: Partir**anno** la settimana prossima.
They're leaving next week.

The Italian future tense is conjugated in the following way (below are the three conjugations in Italian **-ARE, -ERE** and **-IRE**):

Mangiare (to eat)	Credere (to believe)	Partire (to leave)
Io mang**erò**	Io cred**erò**	Io part**irò**
Tu mang**erai**	Tu cred**erai**	Tu part**irai**
Lui/Lei mang**erà**	Lui/Lei cred**erà**	Lui/Lei part**irà**
Noi mang**eremo**	Noi cred**eremo**	Noi part**iremo**
Voi mang**erete**	Voi cred**erete**	Voi part**irete**
Loro mang**eranno**	Loro cred**eranno**	Loro part**iranno**

Examples

ENGLISH: Will + Infinitive Verb.
ITALIAN: Root of Infinitive + correct ending

I will go to run later	**They will go to visit you soon**
Andrò a correre dopo	Verranno presto a visitarvi
You will not finish	**I will study all day**
Voi non finirete	Studierò tutto il giorno
She will call you later	**They will get your food**
Lei ti chiamerà dopo	Prenderanno il tuo cibo
	He will cook for you today
	Lui cucinerà per te oggi

Essere (to be)	Avere (to have)
Io **sarò**	Io **avrò**
Tu **sarai**	Tu **avrai**
Lui/Lei **sarà**	Lui/Lei **avrà**
Noi **saremo**	Noi **avremo**
Voi **sarete**	Voi **avrete**
Loro **saranno**	Loro **avranno**

He will wait for you at 12
Ti aspetterà alle 12
He will fly out at 3
Volerà alle 3
He will wait for you at 12
Ti aspetterà fino alle 12
You will take me home
Mi porterai a casa
You will not be on time
Non sarai puntuale

What is a conditional verb?

The Italian Present Conditional Tense (condizionale presente) is the Italian equivalent to any verb that ends in **"ould" + verb** (for instance: I would run).

How to convert a Italian Verb into a Conditional tense Verb?

Although there are some irregulars instances of the Italian Present Conditional Tense, forming present conditionals is simple: just take any given verb, **drop the infinitive form ARE/ERE/IRE, and add the appropriate endings.**

The endings of the Italian Present Conditional Tense are the same for the –are and –ere conjugations, while –ire is slightly different.

Mangiare (to eat)	Credere (to believe)	Partire (to leave)
Io mang**erei**	Io cred**erei**	Io part**irei**
Tu mang**eresti**	Tu cred**eresti**	Tu part**iresti**
Lui/Lei mang**erebbe**	Lui/Lei cred**erebbe**	Lui/Lei part**irebbe**
Noi mang**eremmo**	Noi cred**eremmo**	Noi part**iremmo**
Voi mang**ereste**	Voi cred**ereste**	Voi part**ireste**
Loro mang**erebbero**	Loro cred**erebbero**	Loro part**irebbero**

Lesson 13: Part 1

EXAMPLES:

English: Conditional	Italiano: Condizionale
Could	Potrei
Should	Dovrei
Would eat	Mangerei
Would call	Chiamerei
Would wait	Aspetterei
Would talk	Parlerei
Would study	Studierei
Would buy	Comprerei
Would take	Porterei

He would try to finish tomorrow if he gets paid
Cercherà di finire domani se riceve il pagamento
I could go to run if the weather is nice
Potrei andare a correre se il tempo è bello
You should come to study only if you are ready for it
Dovresti venire a srudiare solo se sei pronto
I would go to visit you if you would be available for me
Verrei a trovarvi se foste disponibili
We would eat at your place if you would cook for all of us
Mangeremmo a casa vostra se vuoi cucinaste per tutti noi
They would call you at noon if you could have an answer for them
Chiamerebbero a mezzogiorno se voi aveste una risposta per loro
I would take you to the airport if you are ready by 8
Ti porterei all'aeroporto se fossi pronto per le 8
You would be very happy if you co uld just try to lend a hand
Ti sentiresti molto felice, se solo provassi a dare una mano
She would wait for them at noon if they are all showing up
Li aspetterebbe a mezzogionro se venissero tutti
They would prefer if you don't do anything for the moment
Preferirebbero che tu non facessi nulla per il momento

Infinitive V.	Infinito
Can	Potere
Shall	Dovere
To go	Andare
To eat	Mangiare
To call	Chiamare
To wait	Sperare
To talk	Parlare
To study	Studiare
To buy	Comprare
To take	Portare

The South Beach method for conversational Italian

63

"The Four Templates"

Through this method you'll build any phrase with an "Infinitive   Verb
Using the same verbs, let us build some sentences using the   four templates

Gerund/ Gerundio (Action)

To eat = Mangiare; Kill the "are" & add "ando"
Sto mangiando
 I   am   eating

To read = Leggere; kill the "ere" & add "endo"
Lui sta leggendo
He is   reading

Participle/Participio

To eat = Mangiare; kill the "are" & add "ato"
Io ho mangiato
 I have eaten

To sleep = Dormire; kill   the "ire" & add "ito"
Lui ha dormito
He has walked

Future/ Futuro

To eat = Mangiare; Kill "are" & add correct ending
Io mangerò
 I   will   eat

To sleep = Dormire; Kill "ire" & add correct ending
Lui dormirà
He will   sleep

Conditional/Condicional

To eat = Mangiare; kill the "are" & add correct ending
Io mangerei
 I   would eat

To read = Leggere; Kill the "ere" & add correct ending
Lui leggerebbe
He would read

The four templates

"The Infinitive Verbs" are the foundation of this course. Most start with a "To" in English and end with "ARE/ERE/IRE" in Italiano

How to change an Italian " **Infinitive Verb"** into a

Gerund/ Gerundio (Action)	**Participle/Participio (Past Participle)**
ENGLISH: To be + Verb ending in "ing"	ENGLISH: To Have + Participle Verb
ITALIANO: Essere + Verb ending in "ando" o "endo"	ITALIANO: Essere/Avere + Verb ending in "ato","uto","ito"

"Conditional/Condizionale"

ENGLISH: Would+Infinitive ITALIAN: Kill "are/ere/ire" + the correct endings

Mangiare (to eat)	**Credere** (to believe)	**Partire** (to leave)
Io mang**erei**	Io cred**erei**	Io part**irei**
Tu mang**eresti**	Tu cred**eresti**	Tu part**irsti**
Lui/Lei mang**erebbe**	Lui/Lei cred**ererebbe**	Lui/Lei part**irebbe**
Noi mang**eremmo**	Noi cred**eremmo**	Noi part**iremmo**
Voi mang**ereste**	Voi cred**ereste**	Voi part**ireste**
Loro mang**erebbero**	Loro cred**erebbero**	Loro part**irebbero**

Example: To do = fare   **He would do it**   Lo *farebbe*

"Future/ Futuro"

ENGLISH: Will+Infinitive ITALIAN: Kill "are/ere/ire" + the correct endings

Mangiare (to eat)	**Credere** (to believe)	**Partire** (to leave)
Io mang**erò**	Io cred**erò**	Io part**irò**
Tu mang**erai**	Tu cred**erai**	Tu part**irai**
Lui/Lei mang**erà**	Lui/Lei cred**erà**	Lui/Lei part**irà**
Noi mang**eremo**	Noi cred**eremo**	Noi part**iremo**
Voi mang**erete**	Voi cred**erete**	Voi part**irete**
Loro mang**eranno**	Loro cred**eranno**	Loro part**iranno**

Example: To eat = mangiare   **I will eat later**   *Mangerò* dopo

How to change an Italian **"Infinitive Verb"** into a:

" Gerund Verb"
Kill the "are/ere/ire"& add "ando","endo"
Example:

Aspettare becomes Aspettando
I have been waiting for you
Tu stavo aspettando

"Past Participle Verb"
Kill the "are/ere/ire"& add "ato","uto","ito"
Example:

Aspettare becomes Aspettato
I have waited for you all night
Tu ho aspettato tutta la notte

The South Beach method for conversational Italian

The 11 Verbs

We revisit English grammar in order to translate properly from English to Italian

Pay close attention to these 11 verbs because you need proper English to speak proper Italian!

Lesson 14

To be	Essere	To have	Avere	Can	Potere
Could	Potrei	Shall	Dovere	Should	Dovrei
Will	-	Must	Dovere	Might	Potrei
May	Potrei	Would	Vorrei		

These verbs have unique features that we need to be mindful of:

1)   If any other verb follows one of these 11 verbs, there is never a "To" after it.

Examples : In English most of the times a "To" follows a 1st. verb: I have to go – I want to go – I like to go. Not on these 11 verbs: I am going – I can go – I could go – I may go – I will go.

2)   Except for the verbs To Be & To Have the infinitive form of the other 9 verbs is w/o a "To."

Example : Can, May, Shall always start w/o a "To".

3)   When asking a question with these 11 verbs, we don't use "Do" or "Did" at the beginning of the question; simply flip the verb & the noun.

Example : Normally is: Do I want?-Did I have?, But with these 11 verbs we just flip": Am I?-Can I?

4)   When Negating with these 11 verbs, we don't use "Don't" or "Didn't" we simply add "not" after the verb.

Example : Normally is: I don't want – I don't have to. But with these Verbs we negate as follows: I am not coming, You can not go, You have not eaten.

5)   Except for To Be & To Have, these verbs have no conjugations.

Example : I can-He can / I may- He may / we must-they must

Learning Step 10

Questions & Negations

As you'll see both questions and negations are far easier in Italian than in English

Lesson 15

In Italian, <u>Questions are always and only formulated by adding a question mark at the end of the sentence and by changing the tone of your voice.</u>

Examples:

(Do you want to go to eat?)
Vuoi andare a mangiare?

(Do you have to come?)
Devi venire?

(Can I go to visit her?)
Posso andare a trovarla?

(Should she call me?)
Dovrebbe chiamarmi?

In Italian, Negations are <u>always and only formulated by inserting a Non right before the verb.</u>

Examples:

(You do not want to go to eat)
Non vuoi andare a mangiare

(You don´t have to come)
Non devi venire

(I can not go to visit her)
Non posso andare a trovarla

(She should not call me)
Non dovrebbe chiamarmi

Learning Step 11

"There is"

These two words are expressed in Italian through one word:

"C'è" (Che-eh)

Lesson 16

There is/ c'è

There is: c'è

There are: ci sono

There was: c'era

There were: c'erano

There has been: c'è stato

There have been: ci sono stati

There will be: ci saranno

There would be: ci sarebbero

There would have been: ci sarebbero stati

Learning Step 12

"Er-Est-Y"

Learn how these endings are expressed in Italian

Practice them, specially the conjugations!

The Endings Er - Est - Y

Shorter	Più corto	Shortest	Il più corto		
Better	Meglio	Best	Migliore		
Taller	Più alto	Tallest	Il più alto		
Faster	Più veloce	Fastest	Il più veloce	**Examples:**	
Quicker	Più rapido	Quickest	Il più rapido		
Smaller	Più piccolo	Smallest	Il più piccolo	Shorter than = Più basso di	
Slower	Più lento	Slowest	Il più lento	Better than = Meglio di	
Hotter	Più caldo	Hottest	Il più caldo	Taller than = Più alto di	
Colder	Più freddo	Coldest	Il più freddo	Faster than = Più veloce di	
Dumber	Più tonto	Dumbest	Il più tonto		
Fewer	Meno	Fewest	Il minor numero		
Shorty	Piccoletto	As____ as	Tanto__quanto		
Tardy	Ritardatario	More__than	Più __ di		
Weepy	Piagnucoloso				

WHEN THE ENDING -ER- IS APPLIED TO AN INFINITIVE VERB IT CONVERTS IT INTO A PERSON

To drive	= condurre	Driver = conducente
To eat	= mangiare	Eater = mangiatore
To play	= giocare	Player = giocatore
To run	= correre	Runner = corridore
To sleep	= dormire	Sleeper = dormiglione
To write	= scrivere	Writer = scrittore
To read	= leggere	Reader = lettore
To pay	= pagare	Payer = pagatore
To wash	= lavare	Washer = lavatore
To speak	= parlare	Speaker = parlante/oratore

Learning Step 13

The Verb:

To Have

Learn the different grammar rules that apply to it

Practice them, specially the pronunciations!

To Have / Avere

You use the verb "to have" in Italian for many different reasons, like for example to *show possession* or to *express your needs* or as *auxiliary verb*.

1) **Hold/ Ownership:** Examples: I have a headache / Ho mal di testa

                              I have a son / Ho un figlio

2) **Auxiliary verb:**   Examples: I have done it! / L'ho fatto

3) **Tell your age**:   Examples: I am 24 / Ho 24 anni

In Italian **Duty/ Responsibility** is expressed with the verb **Dovere:**

Examples: I have to go / Devo andare

            You have to come / Devi venire

Verb Dovere (Must/have to)

Io	devo
Tu	devi
Lui/lei	deve
Noi	dobbiamo
Voi	dovete
Loro	devono

Hold/ ownership	Auxiliari verb	Tell your age
I have a family	I have eaten too much	You are 40
Ho una famiglia	Ho mangiato troppo	Hai 40 anni

Learning Step 14

The Verb:

To Like

Learn the different grammar rules that apply to it

Practice them, specially the pronunciations!

"Verb To Like"

Verb "PIACERE" To Like

"Like/Enjoy To" (Present)					"Would Like/Enjoy To" (Conditional)				infinitive verb
I	like	it	Mi	Piace	I'd	like	it	Mi	Piacerebbe
You	like	it	Ti	Piace	You'd	like	it	Ti	Piacerebbe
He	likes	it	Gli	Piace	He'd	like	it	Gli	Piacerebbe
She	likes	it	Le	Piace	She'd	like	it	Le	Piacerebbe
We	like	it	Ci	Piace	We'd	like	it	Ci	Piacerebbe
You	like	it	Vi	Piace	You'd	like	it	Vi	Piacerebbe
They	like	it	Gli	Piace	They'd	like	it	Gli	Piacerebbe
It	like	it	Gli	Piace	It'd	like	it	Gli	Piacerebbe

"The Verb To Like"	Verb "PIACERE"
"Like/Enjoy To" (Past Participle)	**"Will Like/Enjoy To" (Future)**
Mi è piacuto	Mi piacerà
Ti è piaciuto	Ti piacerà
Gli è piaciuto	Gli piacerà
Le è piaciuto	Le piacerà
Ci è piaciuto	Ci piacerà
Vi è piaciuto	Vi piacerà
Gli è piaciuto	Gli piacerà

Cosa succederà?	Cosa ti succede?	Mi succede
What will happen?	What happens to you?	It happens to me
Cosa porterai?	Cosa ti succederebbe se…?	Mi succederebbe
What will you bring?	What would happen to you if	It would happen to me
Chi ti porterà?	Cosa ti è successo?	Mi è successo
Who will bring you?	What has happened to you?	It has happened to me
Chi ti verrà a prendere?	Cosa ti succederà?	Mi succederà
Who will pick you up?	What will happen to you?	It will happen to me
Chi ti troverà?	Cosa ti è successo?	Mi è successo
Who will find you?	What has been happening to you?	It has been happening to me
Chi ti taglierà i capelli?	Chi laverà la tua auto?	Mi fa male la testa
Who will cut your hair?	Who will wash your car?	I have a headache
Sembra troppo per me	Portami indietro	Mi porta mia moglie
It seems too much for me	Bring me back	My wife takes me
Comprami un paio di scarpe	Mi piacerebbe un bicchiere di vino	Mi hai deluso
Buy me a pair of shoes	I will like a cup of wine	You failed me
Non mi entra in testa	Ho perso la mia auto	Ho perso il portafoglio
It does not get through my head	I've lost my car	I've lost my wallet
Mi sono dimenticato di chiamarti	Non mi piacciono per nulla	Non mi parla
I forgot to call you	I do not like them at all	She does not talk to me

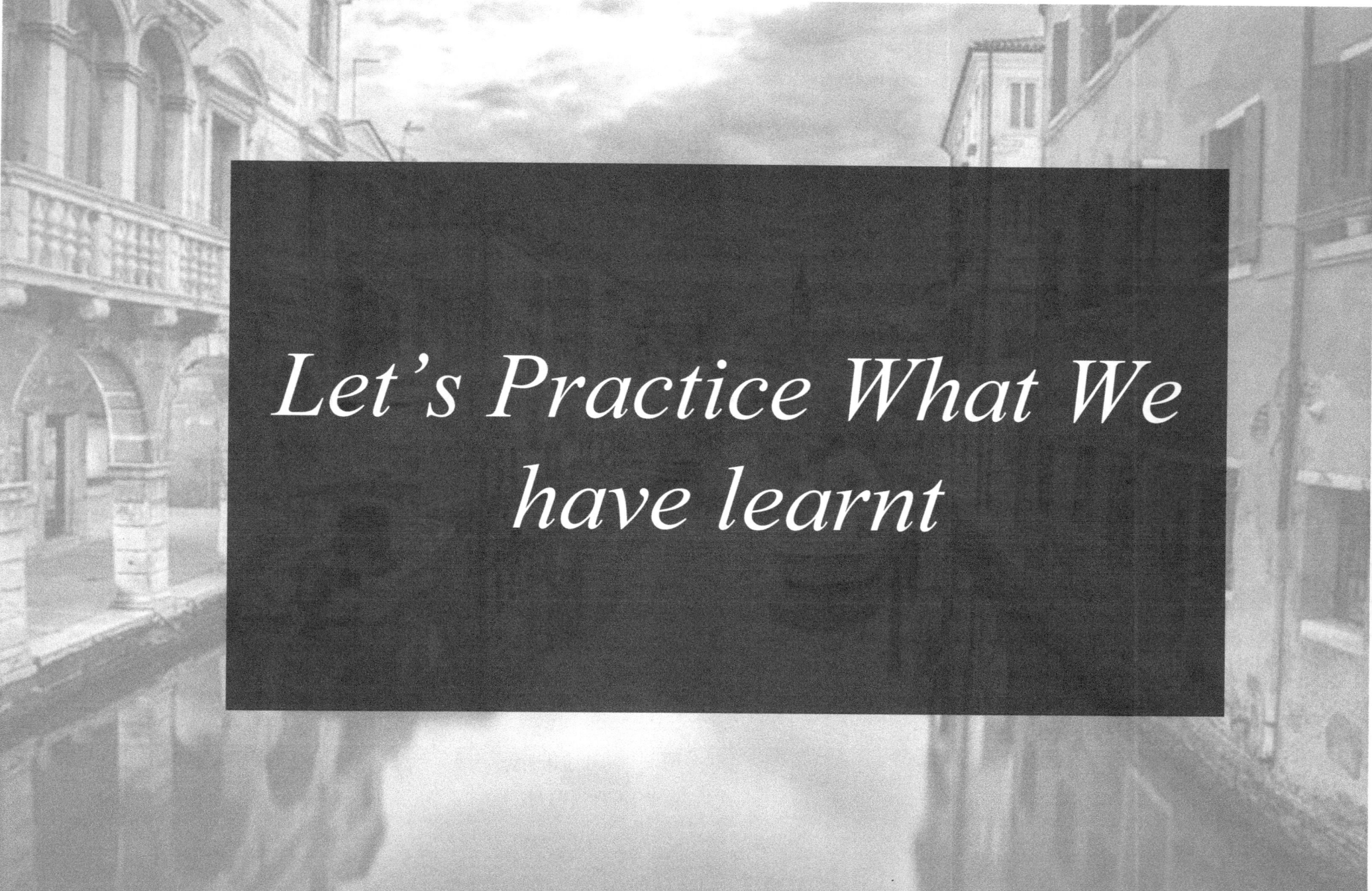

Let's Practice What We have learnt

Infinitives

Example: To Cook (Infinitive Verb) Cucinare

Present	Gerund	Future	Past Particip le	Conditional
I cook	I am cooking	I will cook	I have cooked	I would cook
Io cucino	Io sto cucinando	Io cucinerò	Io ho cucinato	Io cucinerei

I will be cooking		I was cooking	I have to cook	I have been cooking
Io starò cucinando		Io stavo cucinando	Io devo cucinare	Io ho cucinato

I would have cooked	I did cook
Io avrei cucinato	Io cucinai

Example:To Wait (Infinitive Verb) Aspettare

The Four Templates

Present	Gerund	Future	Past Particip le	Conditional
I wait	I am waiting	I will wait	I have waited	I would wait
Io aspetto	Io sto aspettando	Io aspetterò	Io ho aspettato	Io aspetterei

I will be waiting			I have to wait	I have been waiting
Io starò aspettando			Io devo aspettare	Io ho aspettato

I would have waited
Io avrei aspettato

Infinitives (Translate)

Examples: Correre (Infinitive Verb) <u>To run</u>   **The Four Templates**

Present	Gerund	Future	Past Particip le	Conditional
I run	I am running	I will run	I have run	I would run

I will be running   I was running   I have to run   I have been running

I would have run   I ran

Examples: Mangiare (Infinitive Verb) <u>To eat</u>   **The Four Templates**

Present	Gerund	Future	Past Participle	Conditional
I eat	I am eating	I will eat	I have eaten	I would eat

I will be eating   I was eating

I would have eaten   I ate   I have to eat   I have been eating

Infinitives (Translate)

Examples: Parlare (In finitive Verb) To talk

The Four Templates

Present	Gerund	Future	Past Participle	Conditional
I talk	I am talking	I will talk	I have talked	I would talk

I will be talking   I was talking   I have to talk   I have been talking

I would have spoken   I spoke

Exampl es: Chiamare (Infinitive Verb) To call

The Four Templates

Present	Gerund	Future	Past Participle	Conditional
Yo llamo	I am calling	I will call	I have called	I would call

I will be calling   I was calling   I have to call   I have been calling

I would have called   I called

Infinitives (Translate)

Examples: Portare (Infinitive Verb) <u>To take</u>

The Four Templates

Present	Gerund	Future	Past Participle	Conditional
I take	I m taking	I will take	I have taken	I would take
I will be taking	I was taking	I have to take	I have been taking	
I would have taken	I took			

Examples: Ricevere (Infinitive Verb) <u>To get</u>

The Four Templates

Present	Gerund	Future	Past Participle	Conditional
I get	I am getting	I will get	I have gotten	I would get
I will be getting	I was getting	I have to get	I have been getting	
I would have gotten	I got			

Infinitives (Translate)

Examples: Pensare (Infinitive Verb) <u>To think</u>

The Four Templates

Present	Gerund	Future	Past Participle	Conditional
I think	I am thinking	I will think	I have thought	I would think
I will be thinking	I was thinking		I have to think	I have been thinking
I would have thought	I thought			

Examples: Studiare (Infinitive Verb) <u>To study</u>

The Four Templates

Present	Gerund	Future	Past Participle	Conditional
I get	I am getting	I will get	I have gotten	I would get
I will be studying	I was studying		I have to study	I have been studying
I would have studied	I studied			

Infinitives (Translate)

Examples: Scirvere (In finitive Verb) <u>To write</u>   **The Four Templates**

Present	Gerund	Future	Past Participle	Conditional
I write	I am writing	I will write	I have written	I would write

I will be writing   I was writing   I have to write   I have been writing

I would have written   I wrote

Examples: Leggere (Infinitive Verb) <u>To read</u>   **The Four Templates**

Present	Gerund	Futuro	Pasado Participio	Condicional
I read	I am reading	I will read	I have read	I would read

I will be reading   I was reading   I have to read   I have been reading

I would have read   I read

Infinitives (Translate)

Ejemplos: Fare(Infinitive Verb) <u>To Do</u>   The Four Templates

Present	Gerund	Fu ture	Past Particip le	Conditional
I do	I am doing	I will do	I have done	I would do

I will be doing   I was doing   I have to do   I have been doing

I would have done   I did

E xampl es: Lavorare (Infinitive Verb) <u>To Work</u>   The Four Templates

Present	Gerund	Future	Past Particip le	Conditional
I work	I am working	I will work	I have worked	I would work

I will be working   I was working   I have to work   I have been working

I would have worked   I worked

Negation

Examples: <u>To Cook</u> (Infinitive Verb) Cucinare The Four Templates

Present	Gerund	Future	Past Participle	Conditional
I don't cook	I am not cooking	I won't cook	I haven't cooked	I wouldn't cook
Io non cucino	Io non sto cucinando	Io non cucinerò	Io non ho cucinato	Io non cucinerei

I won't be cooking   I wasn't cooking   I don't have to cook   I haven't been cooking
Io non starò cucinando   Io non stavo cucinando   Io non devo cucinare   Io non ho cucinato
I wouldn't have cooked   I didn't cook
Io non avrei cucinato   Io non cucinai

Examples: <u>To Wait</u> (Infinitive Verb) Aspettare The Four Templates

Present	Gerund	Future	Past Participle	Conditional
I don't wait	I am not waiting	I won't wait	I haven't waited	I wouldn't wait
Io non aspetto	Io non sto aspettando	Io non aspetterò	Io non ho aspettato	Io non aspetterei

I won't be waiting   I wasn't waiting   I don't have to wait
Io non starò aspettando   Io non stavo aspettando   Io non devo aspettare
I would not have waited   I did not wait
Io non avrei aspettato   Io non aspettai   I haven't been waiting
                                                   Io non ho aspettato

E xamples: Correre (Infinitive Verb) <u>To Run</u>   The Four Templates

Present	Gerund	Future	Past Particip le	Conditional
I don't run	I am not running	I won' t run	I haven' t run	I wouldn't run

I won' t be running   I wasn't running   I don't have to run   I haven' t been running

I wouldn ' t have run   I didn't run

E xamples: Mangiare (Infinitive Verb) <u>To Eat</u>   The Four Templates

Present	Gerund	Futuro	Past Particip le	Conditional
I don't eat	I am not eating	I won' t eat	I haven' t eaten	I wouldn't eat

I wouldn't be eating   I wasn't eating   I don't have to eat   I haven't been eating

I wouldn ' t have eaten   I didn't eat

Negation (Translate)

Examples: Parlare (Infinitive Verb) <u>To Talk</u>   The Four Templates

Present	Gerund	Future	Past Participle	Conditional
I don't talk	I am not talking	I won' t talk	I haven' t spoken	I wouldn't talk
I won't be talking Y	I wasn't talking	I don't have to talk		I haven't been talking
I wouldn't have spoken	I didn't talk			

Examples: Chiamare (Infinitive Verb) <u>To Call</u>   The Four Templates

Present	Gerund	Future	Past Participle	Conditional
I don't call	I am not calling	I won't call	I haven't called	I wouldn't call
I won't be calling	I wasn't calling	I don't have to call		I haven't been calling
I wouldn't have called	I didn't call			

Negation (Translate)

Examples: Prendere (Infinitive Verb) <u>To Take</u>

The Four Templates

Present	Gerund	Future	Past Participle	Conditional
I don't take	I am not taking	I won't take	I haven't taken	I wouldn't take
I won't be taking	I wasn't taking		I don't have to take	I haven't been taking
I wouldn't have taken	I didn't take			

Examples: Ricevere (Infinitive Verb) <u>To Get</u>

The Four Templates

Present	Gerund	Future	Past Participle	Conditional
I don't get	I am not getting	I won't get	I haven't gotten	I wouldn't get
I wouldn't be getting	I wasn't getting		I don't have to get	I haven't been getting
I wouldn't have gotten	I didn't get			

Examples: Pensare (Infinitive Verb) <u>To Think</u>   The Four Templates

Present	Gerund	Future	Past Participle	Conditional
I don't think	I am not thinking	I wont think	I haven't thought	I wouldn't think

I won' t be thinking   I wasn't thinking   I don't have to think   I haven't been thinking

I wouldn't have been thinking   I didn't think

Examples: Studiare (Infinitive Verb) <u>To Study</u>   The Four Templates

Present	Gerund	Future	Past Participle	Conditional
I don't study	I am not studying	I won't study	I haven't studied	I wouldn't study

I won't be studying   I wasn't studying

I wouldn't have studied   I didn't study   I don't have to study   I haven't been studying

Examples: Scrivere (Infinitive Verb) <u>To Write</u>   The Four Templates

Present	Gerund	Future	Past Participle	Conditional
I don't write	I am not writing	I won't write	I haven't written	I wouldn't write

I won't be writing   I wasn't writing

I don't have to write I haven't been writing

I wouldn't have written   I didn't write

Exampl es: Leggere (Infinitive Verb) <u>To Read</u>   The Four Templates

Present	Gerund	Future	Past Participle	Conditional
I don't write	I am not writing	I won't write	I haven't written	I wouldn't write

I won't be reading   I wasn't reading

I don't have to read   I haven't been reading

I wouldn't have read   I didn't read

Examples: Fare (Infinitive Verb) <u>To Do</u>

The Four Templates

Present	Gerund	Future	Past Participle	Conditional
I don't do	I am not doing	I won't do	I haven't done	I wouldn't do

I won't be doing	I wasn't doing		I don't have to do	I haven't been doing
I wouldn't have done	I didn't do			

Examples: Lavorare (Infinitive Verb) <u>To Work</u>

The Four Templates

Present	Gerund	Future	Past Participle	Conditional
I don't work	**I am not working**	I won't work	I haven't worked	I wouldn't work

I won't be working	I wasn't working			
			I don't have to work	I haven't been working
I wouldn't have worked	I didn't work			

Questions

Example: To <u>Cook</u> (Infinitive Verb) cucinare   **The Four Templates**

Present	**Gerund**	**Future**	**Past Participle**	**Conditional**
Do I cook?	Am I cooking?	Will I cook?	Have I cooked?	Would I cook?
(Io) Cucino?	Sto cucinando?	Cucinerò?	Ho cucinato?	Cucinerei?

Will I be cooking?   Was I cooking?   Do I have to cook?   Have I been cooking?
Starò cucinando   Stavo cucinando?   Devo cuncinare?   Ho cucinato?

Would I have cooked?   Did I cook?
Avrei cucinato?   Cucinai?

Example: To <u>Wait</u> (Infinitive Verb) aspettare   **The Four Templates**

Present	**Gerund**	**Future**	**Past Participle**	**Conditional**
Do I wait?	Am I waiting?	Will I wait?	Have I waited?	Would I wait?
Aspetto?	Sto aspettando?	Aspetterò?	Ho aspettato?	Aspetterei?

Will I be waiting?   Was I waiting?   Do I have to wait?   Have I been waiting?
Scriverò   Stavo scrivendo?   Devo scrivere?   Ho scritto?

Would I have waited?   Did I wait?
Avrei scritto?   Scrissi?

Questions (Translate)

Example: Correre (Infinitive Verb) To Run

The Four Templates

Present	Gerund	Future	Past Participle	Conditional
Do I run?	Am I running?	Will I run?	Have I run?	Will I run?

Will I be running ?	Was I running?			
Would I have run ?	Did I run?		Do I have to run?	Have I been running ?

Example: Mangiare (Infinitive Verb) To eat

The Four Templates

Present	Gerund	Future	Past Participle	Conditional
Do I eat ?	Am I eating?	Will I eat ?	Have I eaten?	Would I eat ?

Will I be eating ?	Was I eating?			
Would I have eaten? ?	Did I eat ?		Do I have to eat?	Have I been eating ?

Example: Hablar (Infinitive Verb) <u>To talk</u>

The Four Templates

Present	**Gerund**	**Future**	**Past Particip le**	**Conditional**
Do I talk ?	Am I talking?	Will I talk ?	Have I talked?	Would I talk ?

Will I be talking ?	Was I talking?		Do I have to talk?	Have I been talking ?
Would I have talked ?	Did I talk ?			

Example: Llamar (Infinitive Verb) <u>To call</u>

The Four Templates

Present	**Gerund**	**Future**	**Past Particip le**	**Conditional**
Do I call?	Am I calling?	Will I call?	Have I called ?	Would I call?

Will I be calling ?	Was I calling?		Did I have to call?	Have I been calling ?
Would I have called ?	Did I call?			

Questions (Translate)

Example: Prendere (Infinitive Verb) <u>To take</u>

The Four Templates

Present	Gerund	Future	Past Particip le	Conditional
Do I take?	Will I take?	Will I take?	Have I taken?	Would I take?

Will I be taking?   Was I taking?

Do I have to take? Have I been taking ?

Would I have taken ?   Did I take?

Example: Ricevere (Infinitive Verb) <u>To get</u>

The Four Templates

Present	Gerund	Future	Past Particip le	Conditional
Do I get ?	Am I getting?	Will I get ?	Have I gotten?	Would I get ?

Have I been getting ?   Was I getting?

Do I have to get?   Have I been getting ?

Would Have I gotten ?   Did I receive ?

Example: Pensare (Infinitive Verb) <u>To think</u>

The Four Templates

Present	Gerund	Future	Past Particip le	Conditional
Do I think ?	Am I thinking?	Will I think ?	Have I thought ?	Would I think ?

Will I be thinking ?

Was I thinking?

Do I have to think?   Have I been thinking ?

Would I have thouhgt ?

Did I ?

Example: Studiare (Infinitive Verb) <u>To study</u>

The Four Templates

Present	Gerund	Future	Past Particip le	Conditional
Do I study ?	Am I studying?	Will I study ?	Have I studied ?	Would I study ?

Will I be studying ?

Was I studying?

Do I have to study?   Have I been studying?

Would have I studied ?

Did I study ?

Questions (Translate)

Example: Scrivere (Infinitive Verb) <u>To write</u>   **The Four Templates**

Present	**Gerund**	**Future**	**Past Particip le**	**Conditional**
Do I write?	Am I writing?	Will I write?	Have I written?	Would I write?

Will I be writing ?   Was I writing?   Do I have to write? Have I been writing ?

Would have I written ?   Did I write?

Example: Leggere (Infinitive Verb) <u>To read</u>   **The Four Templates**

Present	**Gerund**	**Future**	**Past Particip le**	**Conditional**
Do I read?	Am I reading?	Will I read?	Have I read?	Would I read?

Will I be reqading ?   Was I reading?   Do I have to read? Have I been reading ?

Would I have read ?   Did I read?

Example: Fare (Infinitive Verb) <u>To do</u>

The Four Templates

Present	Gerund	Future	Past Particip le	Conditional
Do I do?	Am I doing?	Will I do?	Have I done ?	Would I do?

Will I be doing ?	Was I doing?		Do I have to do?	Have I been doing ?
Would I have done? ?	Did I do?			

Example: Lavorare (Infinitive Verb) <u>To work</u>

The Four Templates

Present	Gerund	Future	Past Particip le	Conditional
Do I work ?	Am I working?	Will I work ?	Have I worked ?	Would I work ?

Will I be working ?	Was I working?		Do I Have to work?	Have I been working ?
Would Have I worked ?	Did I work ?			

Italian Vocabulary

Italian Vocabulary

A

A little: un poco
A: un/uno/una
A lot: molto
About: circa
Above: sopra
Ache: male
Address: indirizzo
Airport: aeroporto
After: dopo
Afternoon: pomeriggio
Afterwards: in seguito
Again: di nuovo
Ago: fa
Aid: aiuto
Air: aria
Airline: linea aerea
Airplane: aereoplano
All: tutto
Almost: quasi
Alone: solo
Already: già
Also: anche
Always: sempre
Amusing: divertente
And: e
Annoy: disturbare
Another: un altro

Anybody: chiunque
Anyone: tutti
Apple: mela
April: aprile
Arrest: arresto
Arrival: arrivo
At (Place): a
At (Hour): alle
Automobile: automobile
Autumn: autunno
Awful: terribile
August: agosto

B

Baggage: valigia
Bad: cattivo
Baked: al forno
Bakery: panificio
Bank: banca
Barely: appena
Bargains: occasioni
Bathroom: bagno
Because: perché
Bed: letto
Bed Cover: copriletto
Beef: manzo
Beer: birra
Behind: dietro
Between: tra
Bicycle: bicicletta

Black: nero
Blood: sangue
Blue: blu
Boat: barca
Book: libro
Boss: capo
Bottle: bottiglia
Box: scatola
Boy: ragazzo
Bread: pane
Breakfast: colazione
British: britannico
Brown: marrone
Bulb: lampadina
Bull: torno
Bus: autobus
Busy: occupato
But: ma
Butter: burro
Button: tasto/pulsante
By the way: a proposito

C

Calf: vitello/polpaccio
Canteen: mensa
Car: auto
Careful: attento
Cart: carrello
Caution: attenzione

Italian Vocabulary

Cents: centesimi
Cereal: cereale
Change: cambio
Cheap: economico
Cheese: formaggio
Cherry: cigliegia
Chest: petto
Chicken: pollo
Child: bambino
Chocolate: cioccolato
Church: chiesa
Cigarette Lighter: accendino
Clean: pulito
Clock: orologio
Clothes: vestiti
Class: classe
Close: chiudere(*verb*)/vicino
Coat: cappotto
Coal: carbone
Coffee: caffé
Cold: freddo
Complete: completare
Concert: concerto
Corner: angolo
Cream: panna
Cup: tazza
Curve: curva
Customs: dogana

D

Daily: quotidiano
Ladies: signore
Dance: danza
Danger: pericolo
Dark: scuro
Day: giorno
Dead: morto
Dear: caro
December: dicembre
Dentist: dentista
Department Store: grande magazzino
Departure: partenza
Dinner: cena
Discount: sconto
Desert: deserto
Despite: nonostante
Dessert: dolce
Detour: deviazione
Diapers: pannolini
Dictionary: dizionario
Dining room: sala da pranzo
Dirty: sporco
Dizzy: vertiginoso
Down: giù
Dozen: dozzina
Dress: abito
Drip (Leak): gocciolamento
Drugstore: farmacia

E

Each: ogni
Early: presto
Egg: uovo
Either: o/entrambi
Electricity: elettricità
Eleven: undici
Embassy: ambasciata
Emergency: emergenza
Empty: vuoto
England: Inghilterra
Entrance: entrata
Error: errore
Evening: sera
Even though: nonostante
Every: ogni
Everybody: tutti
Exchange: scambio
Excursion: escursione
Excuse (me): mi scusi
Exit: uscita
Expensive: caro
Eye: occhio
Eye Glasses: occhiali

F

Fair: equo
Family: famiglia
Far: lontano

Fast: veloce
Father: padre
Faucet: rubinetto
Fault: colpa
February: febbraio
Fever: febbre
Film: film/pellicola
Fine: bene
Fire: fuoco
First: primo
Fish: pesce
Flag: bandiera
Flight: volo
Fly: volare(*verb*)/mosca
Food: cibo
Foot: piede
For: per
Forbidden: vietato
Fork: forchetta
Forty: quaranta
Four: quattro
Fourteen: quattordici
Fourth: quarto
Free: libero
Fresh water: acqua fresca
Friday: venerdì
Fried: fritto
Friend: amico
Friendly: amichevole

From: da
Fruit: frutta
Funny: divertente

G

Game: gioco
Garlic: aglio
Gas: gas
Gasoline: benzina
Generally: generalmente
Gentleman: gentiluomo
Gift: regalo
Girl: ragazza
Glove: guanto
Good: buono
Gray: grigio
Green: verde
Greetings: saluti
Guide: guida

H

Half: metà
Ham: prosciutoo
Handbag: borsetta
Happy: felice
Headache: mal di testa
Heart: cuore
Heat: calore
Heavy: pesante
Hello: ciao

Help: aiuto
Here: qui
Hospital: ospedale
Hot: caldo
Hour: ora
How: come
How far: quanto lontano
How long: per quanto
How much: quanto
Hot: caldo
Hundred: cento
Husband: marito

I

Ice cream: gelato
If: se
Immediately: immediatamente
In: a/in
Included: incluso
Infant: neonato
Information: informazione
Inside: dentro
Introduce: presentare

J

Jam: marmellata
January: gennaio
Jewelry: gioielleria
Juice: succo
July: luglio

Italian Vocabulary

K
Keep: tenere
Key: chiave
Kind: gentile
Kitchen: cucina
Knife: coltello

L
Lady: signora
Large: grande
Last: ultimo
Late: tardi
Lavatory: gabinetto
Laxative: lassativo
Least: meno
Leather: pelle
Left: sinistra
Legal: legale
Lemon: limone
Lemonade: limonata
Less: meno
Letter: lettera
Lettuce: lattuga
List: lista
Little: piccolo
Low: basso
Lunch: pranzo

N
Nothing: niente
Notice: avviso
November: novembre
Now: ora
Number: numero

M
Machine: macchina
Madam: signora
Made in: fatto in
Magazine: rivista
Mail: posta
Manager: direttore
Many: molti
Map: mappa
March: marzo
Matches: fiammiferi
May: maggio
May be: può essere
Meal: pasto
Men: uomini
Merely: semplicemente
Meat: carne
Menu: menu
Message: messaggio
Middle: centrale
Midnight: mezzanotte
Milk: latte

Minute: minuto
Miss: Sig.na
Mister: Signor
Monday: lunedì
Money: denaro
Money Order: vaglia
Month: mese
Morning: mattino
Mother: madre
Motorcycle: motocicletta
Movie: film
Mr.: Sig.
Mrs.: Sig.ra
Much: molto
Museum: museo

N
Napkin: tovagliolo
Nationality: nazionalità
Naturally: naturalmente
Near: vicino
Neither: nessuno dei due
Never: mai
Next: prossimo
Next to: vicino a
Night: notte
Nightclub: locale notturno
Nine: nove
Nineteen: diciannove
Ninety: novanta

Italian Vocabulary

Ninth: nono
No: no
Noise: rumore
None: nessuno
Noon: pomeriggio
Not: non

O

October: ottobre
Of course: di certo
Office: ufficio
Often: spesso
Okay: ok
Omelet: frittata
On: su/acceso
Once: una volta
One: uno
One Hundred: cento
Only: solo
On sale: in vendita
Open: aprire
Orange: arancione
Otherwise: altrimenti
Outside: fuori
Over: oltre
Overcoat: cappotto

P

Pack: pacco
Page: pagina

Pain: dolore
Paint: vernice
Pan: padella
Paper: carta
Parent: genitori
Park: parco
Part: parte
Partly: parzialmente
Past: passato
People: gente
Payment: pagamento
Phone: telefono
Pink: rosa
Player: giocatore
Pleasure: piacere
Polite: gentile
Pollution: inquinamento
Poor: povero
Pregnant: incinta
Present: presente/regalo
Previous: precedente

Q

Queen: regina
Question: domanda
Quick: veloce
Quite: abbastanza

R

Radiator: termosifone

Railroad: ferrovia
Rain: pioggia
Raincoat: impermeabile
Razor Blade: lama del rasoio
Ready: pronto
Receipt: ricevuta
Record: registrazione/disco
Red: rosso
Repeat: ripetere
Reserved: prenotato
Rest Room: bagno
Rice: riso
Right: giusto/destra
Right away: subito
Right now: proprio ora
Roast Beef: arrosto di manzo
Roasted: arrostito
Round Trip: andata e ritorno

S

Salad: insalata
Sale: vendita
Salty: salato
Saturday: sabato
School: scuola
Seat: posto a sedere
Second: secondo
See you later: a dopo
September: settembre

Italian Vocabulary

Service: servizio
Seven: sette
Seventh: settimo
Seventeen: diciassette
Seventy: settanta
Several: parecchi
Ship: nave
Shopping: shopping
Show Me: mostrami
Shower: doccia
Shrimp: gamberetto
Sick: malato
Sir: Sig.
Six: sei
Sixteen: sedici
Sixth: sesto
Sixty: sessanta
Slow: lento
Small: piccolo
Smoker: fumatore
Snack: merenda
Soap: sapone
Soon: presto
Soup: minestra
Somebody: qualcuno
Someone: qualcuno
Spoon: cucchiaio

Sports: sport
Spring: molla
Spring (season): primavera
Station: stazione
Stewardess: hostess
Sticker: etichetta
Still: ancora/fermo
Stop: fermare
Store: negozio
Strawberry: fragola
Street: strada
Subway: metropolitana
Sugar: zucchero
Suitcase: valigia
Summer: estate
Sunday: domenica
Sure: sicuro
T
Table: tavolo
Tablet: tablet/compressa
Tailor: sarto
Tap: rubinetto
Tea: té
Teaspoon: cucchiaino
Telegram: telegramma
Telephone: telefono
Television: televisione
Ten: dieci

Thank you: grazie
Theft: furto
There: là
There is/are: c'è/ci sono
Thermometer: termometro
Thief: ladro
Thing: cosa
Third: terzo
Thirteen: tredici
Thirty: trenta
This evening: questo pomeriggio
Thousand: mille
Three: tre
Through: attraverso
Thursday: giovedì
Tuesday: martedì
Ticket: biglietto
Time (Hour): ora
Timetable: orario
Tip (gratuity): mancia
To: a
Toast (bread): toast
Tabacco: tabacco
Today: oggi
Toilet paper: carta igienica
Toilet: gabinetto
Tomorrow: domani
Tonight: questa sera
Too (Also): anche

Italian Vocabulary

Tourism: turismo
Tourist: turista
Towel: asciugamano
Track: traccia
Traffic: traffico
Train: treno
Tuesday: martedì
TV Set: televisiore
Twelve: dodici
Twenty: venti
Twice: due volte
Two: due
Two hundred: duecento
Typewriter: macchina da scrivere

U
Umbrella: ombrello
Under: sotto
Underneath: al di sotto
Understood: capito
United States: Stati Uniti
Until: fino
Up: su
Urgent: urgente
Unless: a meno che
Unwilling: riluttante

V
Vacant: libero/disponibile
Valuable: prezioso

Vanilla: vaniglia
Veal: vitello
Vegetables: verdure
Very: molto
Vinegar: aceto

W
Waiter: cameriere
Waitress: cameriera
Waiting Room: sala d'attesa
Wallet: portafoglio
Warm: caldo
Watch out: fare attenzione
Water: acqua
Watermelon: anguria
Wednesday: mercoledì
Week: settimana
Weekly: settimanalmente
Welcome: benvenuto
Well: bene
Wet paint: vernice fresca
What: cosa
When: quando
Whenever: ogni volta
Where: dove
Where to: dove
Wherever: dovunque
Which: quale

Whichever: qualunque cosa
White: bianco
Who: chi
Whoever: chiunque
Whom: chi
Whose: di chi
Why: perché
Wide: ampio
Wife: sposa
Willing: disposto
Window: finestra
Wine: vino
Winter: inverno
With: con
Woman: donna
Women: donne
Word: parola
Wristwatch: orologio da polso

Y
Year: anno
Yellow: giallo
Yes: sì
Yesterday: ieri
Yet: già
Yield: resa/rendimento

Z
Zipper: cerniera

Notes

1- <u>Gerund / (Gerundio):</u> In English verbs in Gerund require the verb "To Be" to precede them, in Italian they use the verb " Stare", To Stay. To practice building phrases in Gerund (Action), simply place the Verb To Stay ("Stare") just before the Gerund Verb using the following conjugations.

(I – stay) –	Io sto
(You – stay) –	Tu stai
(He – stays) –	Lui sta
(She – stays) –	Lei sta
(We – stay) –	Noi stiamo
(You – stay) –	Voi state
(They – stay) –	Loro stanno
(It – stays) –	(esso) sta

Examples:

I Am Writing	Io sto scrivendo
You Are Waiting	Tu stai scrivendo
He is Calling	Lui sta chiamando
She Is Cooking	Lei sta cucinando
We Are Eating	Noi stiamo mangiando
You Are Eating	Voi state mangiando
They Are Coming	Loro stanno mangiando

2-Participle (Participio): in Italian *Compound verbs* require the verb "Avere" (To have) or "Essere" (To be) to precede the past participle. Transitive verbs mostly take *Avere* as auxiliary verb; verbs of movement, reflexive and reciprocal verbs, and some other intransitive verbs use *Essere*. To practice building phrases in the Past, simply place the Verb To Have ("Avere") or to be ("Essere") just before the Participle Verb using the following conjugations:

(I – Am) –	Io sono	(I – have)	Io ho
(You – Are) –	Tu sei	(You - have)	Tu hai
(He – is) –	Lui è	(He – has)	Lui ha
(She – is) –	Lei è	(She – has)	Lei ha
(We – Are) –	Noi siamo	(We – have)	Noi abbiamo
(You – Are) –	Voi siete	(You – have)	Voi avete
(They – Are) –	Loro sono	(They – have)	Loro hanno
(IT – is) –	(esso) è	(It – has)	(esso) ha

Examples:

I have Waited	Io ho aspettato
You Have Gotten Mail	Tu hai ricevuto una email
She Has Slept Well	Lei ha dormito bene
He Has Eaten Late	Lui ha mangiato tardi
We have run in the morning	Noi abbiamo corso questa mattina
You have gone to class early	Voi siete andati a lezione presto
They Have done the Homework together	Loro hanno fatto i compiti insieme

Notes

In Italian you use the letter "A" between infinitive verbs.

Examples:
I can go to eat later
 Posso andare a mangiare dopo

I want to come to visit you next week
Voglio venire a trovarti la prossima settimana

 I have to go to eat
Devo andare a mangiare

Appendix

Answers to page 83:

Verb <u>*To run: Correre;*</u> <u>I run</u>: Io corro, <u>I am running</u>: Io sto correndo, <u>I will run</u>: Io correrò, <u>I have run</u>: Io ho corso, <u>I would run</u>: Io vorrei correre, <u>I will be running</u>: Io starò correndo, <u>I was running</u>: Io stavo correndo, <u>I have to run</u>: Io devo correre, <u>I have been running</u>: Io ho corso, <u>I would have run</u>: Io avrei corso, <u>I ran</u>: Io corsi

Verb <u>*To eat: Mangiare*</u>; <u>I eat</u>: Io mangio, <u>I am eating</u>: Io stavo mangiano, <u>I will eat</u>: Io manger, <u>I have eaten</u>: Io ho mangiato, <u>I would eat</u>: Io mangerei, <u>I will be eating</u>: Io starò mangiando, <u>I was eating</u>: Io stavo mangiando, <u>I have to eat</u>: Io devo mangiare, <u>I have been eating</u>: Io ho mangiato, <u>I would have eaten</u>: Io avrei mangiato, <u>I ate</u>: Io mangiai

Answers to page 84:

Verb <u>*To Talk: Parlare;*</u> <u>I speak</u>: Io parlo, <u>I am speaking</u>: Io sto parlando, <u>I will speak</u>: Io parlerò, <u>I have spoken</u>: Io ho parlato, <u>I would speak</u>: Io parlerei, <u>I will be talking</u>: Io starò parlando, <u>I was talking</u>: Io stavo parlando, <u>I have to talk</u>: Io devo parlare, <u>I have been talking</u>: Io ho parlato, <u>I would have spoken</u>: Io avrei parlato, <u>I spoke</u>: Io parlay

Verb <u>*To Call: Chiamare,*</u> <u>I call</u>: Io chiamo, <u>I am calling</u>: Io sto chiamando, <u>I will call</u>: Io chiamerò, <u>I have called</u>: Io ho chiamato, <u>I would call</u>: Io chiamerei, <u>I will be calling</u>: Io starò chiamando, <u>I was calling</u>: Io stavi, <u>I have to call</u>: Io devo chiamare chiamando, <u>I have been calling</u>: Io ho chiamato, <u>I would have called</u>: Io avrei chiamato, <u>I called</u>: Io chiamai

Answers to page 85:

Verb <u>*To Take: Portare;*</u> <u>I take</u>: Io porto, <u>I am taking</u>: Io sto portando, <u>I will take</u>: Io porterò, <u>I have taken</u>: Io ho preso, <u>I would take</u>: Io prenderei, <u>I will be taking</u>: Io starò prendendo, <u>I was taking</u>: Io stavo prendendo, <u>I have to take</u>: Io devo prendere, <u>I have been taking</u>: Io ho preso, <u>I would have taken</u>: Io avrei preso, <u>I took</u>: Io presi

Verb *To Get: Ricevere;* <u>I get</u>: Io ricevo, <u>I am getting</u>: Io sto ricevendo, <u>I will get</u>: Io riceverò, <u>I have gotten</u>: Io ho ricevuto, <u>I would get</u>: Io riceverei, <u>I will be getting</u>: Io starò ricevendo, <u>I was getting</u>: Io stavo ricevendo, <u>I have to get</u>: Io devo ricevere, <u>I have been getting</u>: Io ho ricevuto, <u>I would have gotten</u>: Io avrei ricevuto, <u>I got</u>: Io ricevetti

Answers to page 86:

Verb *To Think: Pensare;* <u>I think</u>: Io penso, <u>I am thinking</u>: Io sto pensando, <u>I will think</u>: Io penserò, <u>I have thought</u>: Io ho pensato, <u>I would think</u>: Io penserei, <u>I will be thinking</u>: Io starò pensando, <u>I was thinking</u>: Io stavo pensando, <u>I have to think</u>: Io devo pensare, <u>I have been thinking</u>: Io ho pensato, <u>I would have thought</u>: Io avrei pensato, <u>I thought</u>: Io pensai

Verb *To Study: Studio,* <u>I study</u>: Io studio, <u>I am studying</u>: Io sto studiando, <u>I will study</u>: Io studierò, <u>I have studied</u>: Io ho studiato, <u>I would study</u>: Io studierei, <u>I will be studying</u>: Io stavo studiando, <u>I was studying</u>: Io stavo studiando, <u>I have to study</u>: Io devo studiare, <u>I have been studying</u>: Io ho studiato, <u>I would have studied</u>: Io avrei studiato, <u>I studied</u>: Io studiai

Answers to page 87:

Verb *To Write: Scrivere;* <u>I write</u>: Io scrivo, <u>I am writing</u>: Io sto scrivendo, <u>I will write</u>: Io scriverò, <u>I have written</u>: Io ho scritto, <u>I would write</u>: Io scriverei, <u>I will be writing</u>: Io starò scrivendo, <u>I was writing</u>: Io stavo scrivendo, <u>I have to write</u>: Io devo scrivere, <u>I have been writing</u>: Io ho scritto, <u>I would have written</u>: Io avrei scritto, <u>I wrote</u>: Io scrissi

Verb *To Read: Leggere;* I read: Io leggo, I am reading: Io sto leggendo, I will read: Io leggerò, I have read: Io ho letto, I would read: Io leggerei, I will be reading: Io starò leggendo, I was reading: Io stavo leggendo, I have to read: Io devo leggere, I have been reading: Io ho letto, I would have read: Io avrei letto, I read: Io lessi

Answers to page 88:

Verb _To Do_: _Fare,_ <u>I do:</u> Io faccio, <u>I am doing:</u> Io sto facendo, <u>I will do:</u> Io farò, <u>I have done:</u> Io ho fatto, <u>I would do:</u> Io farei, <u>I will be doing:</u> Io starò facendo, <u>I was doing:</u> Io stavo facendo, <u>I have to do:</u> Io devo fare, <u>I have been doing:</u> Io ho fatto, <u>I would have done:</u> Io avrei fatto, <u>I did:</u> Io feci

Verb _To Work:_ _Lavorare;_ <u>I work:</u> Io lavoro, <u>I am working:</u> Io sto lavorando, <u>I will work:</u> Io lavorerò, <u>I have worked:</u> Io ho lavorato, <u>I would work:</u> Io lavorerei, <u>I will be working:</u> Io starò lavorando, <u>I was working:</u> Io stavo lavorando, <u>I have to work:</u> Io devo lavorare, <u>I have been working:</u> Io ho lavorato, <u>I would have worked:</u> Io avrei lavorato, <u>I worked:</u> Io lavorai

Answers to page 90:

Verb _To Run:_ _Correre;_ <u>I don't run:</u> Io non corro, <u>I am not running:</u> Io non sto correndo, <u>I won' t run:</u> Io non correrò, <u>I haven' t run:</u> Io non ho corso, <u>I wouldn't run:</u> Io non correrei, <u>I won' t be running:</u> Io non starò correndo, <u>I wasn't running:</u> Io non stavo correndo, <u>I don't have to run:</u> Io non devo correre, <u>I haven' t been running:</u> Io non ho corso, <u>I wouldn't have run:</u> Io non avrei corso, <u>I didn't run:</u> Io non corsi

Verb _To Eat_: _Mangiare;_ <u>I don't eat:</u> Io non mangio, <u>I am not eating:</u> Io non sto mangiando, <u>I won' t eat:</u> Io non mangerò, <u>I haven' t eaten:</u> Io non ho mangiato, <u>I wouldn't eat:</u> Io non mangerei, <u>I wouldn't be eating:</u> Io non starò mangiando, <u>I wasn't eating:</u> Io non stavo mangiando, <u>I don't have to eat:</u> Io non devo mangiare, <u>I haven't been eating:</u> Io non ho mangiato, <u>I wouldn't have eaten:</u> Io non avrei mangiato, <u>I didn't eat:</u> Io non mangiai

Appendix

Answers to page 91:

Verb _To Talk: Parlare;_ <u>I don't talk</u>: Io non parlo, <u>I am not talking:</u> Io non sto parlando, <u>I won' t talk:</u> Io non parlerò, <u>I haven' t spoken</u>: Io non ho parlato, <u>I wouldn't talk</u>: Io non parlerei, <u>I won't be talking</u>: Io non starò parlando, <u>I wasn't talking</u>: Io non stavo parlando, <u>I don't have to talk</u>: Io non devo parlare, <u>I haven't been talking</u>: Io non ho parlato, <u>I wouldn't have spoken</u>: Io non avrei parlato, <u>I didn't talk</u>: Io non parlay

Verb _To Call: Chiamare;_ <u>I don't call</u>: Io non chiamo, <u>I am not calling</u>: Io non soto chiamando, <u>I won't call</u>: Io non chiamerò, <u>I haven't called</u>: Io non ho chiamato, <u>I wouldn't call</u>: Io non chiamerei, <u>I won't be calling</u>: Io non starò chiamando, <u>I wasn't calling</u>: Io non stavo chimanado, <u>I don't have to call</u>: Non devo chiamare, <u>I haven't been calling</u>: Io non ho chiamato, <u>I wouldn't have called</u>: Io non avrei chiamatto, <u>I didn't call</u>: Io non chiamai

Answers to page 92:

Verb _To Take: Prendere;_ <u>I don't take</u>: Io non prendo, <u>I am not taking:</u> Io non sto prendendo, <u>I won't take</u>: Io non prenderò, <u>I haven't taken</u>: Io non ho preso, <u>I wouldn't take</u>: Io non prenderei, <u>I won't be taking</u>: Io non starò prendendo, <u>I wasn't taking:</u> Io non stavo prendendo, <u>I don't have to take</u>: Io non devo prendere, <u>I haven't been taking:</u> Io non ho preso, <u>I wouldn't have taken</u>: Io non avrei preso, <u>I didn't take</u>: Io non presi

Verb _To Get: Ricevere;_ <u>I don't get</u>: Io non ricevo, <u>I am not getting</u>: Io non sto ricevendo, <u>I won't get</u>: Io non riceverò, <u>I haven't gotten</u>: Io non ho ricevuto, <u>I wouldn't get</u>: Io non riceverei, <u>I wouldn't be getting</u>: Io non starò ricevendo, <u>I wasn't getting</u>: Io non stavo ricevendo, <u>I don't have to get:</u> Io non devo ricevere, <u>I haven't been getting</u>: Io non ho ricevuto, <u>I wouldn't have gotten</u>: Io non avrei ricevuto: <u>I didn't get</u>: Io non ricevetti

Answers to page 93:

Verb _To Think: Pensare;_ <u>I don't think</u>: Io non penso, <u>I am not thinking</u>: Io non sto pensando, <u>I won't think</u>: Io non penserò, <u>I haven't thought</u>: Io non ho pensato, <u>I wouldn't think</u>: Io non penserei, <u>I won' t be thinking</u>: Io non starò pensando, <u>I wasn't thinking</u>: Io stavo pensando, <u>I don't have to think</u>: Io non devo pensare, <u>I haven't been thinking</u>: Io non ho pensato, <u>I wouldn't have thought</u>: Io non avrei pensato, <u>I didn't think</u>: Io non pensai

Verb _To Study; Studiare;_ <u>I don't study</u>:Io non studio, <u>I am not studying</u>: Io non sto studiando, <u>I won't study</u>: Io non studierò, <u>I haven't studied</u>: Io non ho studiato, <u>I wouldn't study</u>: Io non studierei, <u>I won't be studying</u>: Io non studierò, <u>I wasn't studying</u>: Io non stavo studiando, <u>I don't have to study</u>: Io non devo studiare, <u>I haven't been studying</u>: Io non ho studiato, <u>I wouldn't have studied</u>: Io non avrei studiato, <u>I didn't study</u>: Io non studiai

Answers to page 94:

Verb _To Write: Scrivere;_ <u>I don't write</u>: Io non scrivo, <u>I am not writing</u>: Io non sto scrivendo, <u>I won't write</u>: Io non scriverò, <u>I haven't written</u>: Io non ho scritto, <u>I wouldn't write</u>: Io non scriverei, <u>I won't be writing</u>: Io non starò scrivendo, <u>I wasn't writing</u>: Io non stavo scrivendo, <u>I don't have to write</u>: Io non devo scrivere, <u>I haven't been writing</u>: Io non ho scritto, <u>I wouldn't have written</u>: Io non avrei scritto, <u>I didn't write</u>: Io non scrissi

Verb _To Read: Leggere;_ <u>I don't read</u>: Io non leggo, <u>I am not reading</u>: Io non sto leggendo, <u>I won't read</u>: Io non leggerò, <u>I haven't read</u>: Io non ho letto, <u>I wouldn't read</u>: Io non leggerei, <u>I won't be reading</u>: Io non starò leggendo, <u>I wasn't reading</u>: Io non stavo leggendo, <u>I don't have to read</u>: Io non devo leggere, <u>I haven't been reading</u>: Io non ho letto, <u>I wouldn't have read</u>: Io non avrei letto, <u>I didn't read</u>: Io non lessi

Appendix

Answers to page 95:

Verb *To Do*: *Fare*; <u>I don't do</u>: Io non faccio, <u>I am not doing</u>: Io non sto facendo, <u>I won't do</u>: Io non farò, <u>I haven't done</u>: Io non ho fatto, <u>I wouldn't do</u>: Io non farei, <u>I won't be doing</u>: Io non starò facendo, <u>I wasn't doing</u>: Io non stavo facendo, <u>I don't have to do</u>: Io non devo fare, <u>I haven't been doing</u>: Io non ho fatto, <u>I wouldn't have done</u>: Io non avrei fatto, <u>I didn't do</u>: Io non feci

Verb *To Work*; *Lavorare*; <u>I don't work</u>: Io non lavoro, <u>I am not working</u>: Io non sto lavorando, <u>I won't work</u>: Io non lavorerò, <u>I haven't worked</u>: Io non ho lavorato, <u>I wouldn't work</u>: Io non lavorerei, <u>I won't be working</u>: Io non starò lavorando, <u>I wasn't working</u>: Io non stavo lavorando, <u>I don't have to work</u>: Io non devo lavorare, <u>I haven't been working</u>: Io non ho lavorato, <u>I wouldn't have worked</u>: Io non avrei lavorato, <u>I didn't work</u>: Io non lavorai

Answers to page 97:

Verb *To Run*: *Correre*; <u>Do I run?</u>: Corro?, <u>Am I running?</u>: Sto correndo?, <u>Will I run?</u>: Correrò?, <u>Have I run?</u>: Ho corso?, <u>Will I run?</u>: Correrò?, <u>Will I be running?</u>: Starò correndo, <u>Was I running?</u>: Stavo correndo?, <u>Do I have to run?</u>: Devo correre?, <u>Have I been running?</u>: Ho corso?, <u>Would I have run?</u>: Avrei corso?, <u>Did I run?</u>: Corsi?

Verb *To Eat*; *Manigare*; <u>Do I eat?</u>: Mangio?, <u>Am I eating?</u>: Sto mangiando?, <u>Will I eat?</u>: Mangerò?, <u>Have I eaten?</u>: Ho mangiato?: <u>Would I eat?</u>: Mangerei?, <u>Will I be eating?</u>: Starò mangiando?, <u>Was I eating?</u>: Stavo mangiando?, <u>Do I have to eat?</u>: Devo mangiare?, <u>Have I been eating?</u>: Ho mangiato?, <u>Would I have eaten?</u>: Avrei mangiato, <u>Did I eat?</u>: Mangiai?

Answers to page 98:

Verb *To Talk: Parlare;* <u>Do I talk?:</u> Parlo?, <u>Am I talking?:</u> Sto parlando?, <u>Will I talk?:</u> Parlerò?, <u>Have I talked?:</u> Ho parlato?, <u>Would I talk?:</u> Parlerei?: <u>Will I be talking?:</u> Starò parlando?, <u>Was I talking?:</u> Stavo parlando?, <u>Do I have to talk?:</u> Devo parlare?, <u>I've been talking?:</u> Ho parlato?, <u>Would I have talked?:</u> Avrei parlato?, <u>Did I talk?:</u> Parlai?

Verb *To Call: Chiamare;* <u>Do I call?:</u> Chiamo?, <u>Am I calling?:</u> Sto chiamando?, <u>Will I call?:</u> Chiamerò?, <u>Have I called?:</u> Devo chiamare?, <u>Would I call?:</u> Chiamerei?, <u>Will I be calling?:</u> Starò chiamando?, <u>Was I calling?:</u> Stavo chiamando, <u>Did I have to call?:</u> Dovevo chiamare?, <u>Have I been calling?:</u> Ho chiamato?, <u>Would I have called?:</u> Avrei chiamato?, <u>Did I call?:</u> Chiamai?

Answers to page 99:

Verb *To Take: Prendere;* <u>Do I take?:</u> Prendo?, <u>Am I taking?:</u> Sto prendendo?, <u>Will I take?:</u> Prenderò, <u>Have I taken?:</u> Ho preso?, <u>Would I take?:</u> Prenderei?, <u>Will I be taking?:</u> Starò prendendo?, <u>Was I taking?:</u> Stavo prendendo?, <u>Do I have to take?:</u> Devo prendere?, <u>Have I been taking?:</u> Ho preso?, <u>Would I have taken?:</u> Avrei preso?, <u>Did I take?:</u> Presi?

Verb *To Get: Ricevere;* <u>Do I get?:</u> Ricevo?, <u>Am I getting?:</u> Sto ricevendo?, <u>Will I get?:</u> Riceverò?, <u>Have I gotten?:</u> Ho ricevuto?, <u>Would I get?;</u> Riceverei?, <u>Will I be getting?:</u> Starò ricevendo?, <u>Was I getting?:</u> Stavo ricevendo?, <u>Do I have to get?:</u> Devo ricevere?, <u>Have I been getting?:</u> Ho ricevuto?, <u>Would Have I gotten?:</u> Avrei ricevuto, <u>Did I get?:</u> Ricevetti?

Appendix

Answers to page 100:

Verb _To Think_: _Pensare;_ <u>Do I think?:</u> Prendo?, <u>Am I thinking?:</u> Sto pensando?, <u>Will I think?:</u> Penserò?, <u>Have I thought?:</u> Ho pensato?, <u>Would I think?:</u> Pesnerei?, <u>Will I be thinking?:</u> Starò pensando?, <u>Was I thinking?:</u> Stavo pensando?, <u>Do I have to think?:</u> Devo pensare?, <u>Have I been thinking?:</u> Ho pensato?, <u>Would I have thought?:</u> Avrei pensato?: <u>Did I think?:</u> Pensai?

Verb _To Study; Studiare;_ <u>Do I study?:</u> Penso?, <u>Am I studying?:</u> Sto studiando?, <u>Will I study?:</u> Studierò?, <u>Have I studied?:</u> Ho studiato?, <u>Would I study?:</u> Studierai?, <u>Will I be studying?:</u> Starò studiando?, <u>Was I studying?:</u> Stavo studiando?, <u>Do I have to study?:</u> Devo studiare, <u>Have I been studying?:</u> Ho studiato?, <u>Would have I studied?:</u> Avrei studiato?, <u>Did I study?:</u> Studiai?

Answers to page 101:

Verb _To Write: Scrivere;_ <u>Do I write?:</u> Scrivo?, <u>Am I writing?:</u> Sto scrivendo?, <u>Will I write?:</u> Scriverò?, <u>Have I written?:</u> Ho scritto?, <u>Would I write?:</u> Scriverei?, <u>Will I be writing?:</u> Starò scrivendo?, <u>Was I writing?:</u> Stavo scrivendo?, <u>Do I have to write?:</u> Devo scrivere?, <u>Have I been writing?:</u> Ho scritto?, <u>Would have I written?:</u> Avrei scritto?, <u>Did I write?:</u> Scrivetti?

Verb _To Read: Leggere;_ <u>Do I read?:</u> Leggo?, <u>Am I reading?:</u> Sto leggendo?, <u>Will I read?:</u> Leggerò?, <u>Have I read?:</u> Ho letto?, <u>Would I read?:</u> Leggerei?, <u>Will I be reading?:</u> Starò leggendo?, <u>Was I reading?:</u> Stavo leggendo?, <u>Do I have to read?:</u> Devo leggere?, <u>Have I been reading?:</u> Ho letto?, <u>Would I have read?:</u> Avrei letto?, <u>Did I read?:</u> Lessi

Answers to page 102:

Verb <u>*To Do: Fare;*</u> <u>Do I do?</u>: Faccio?, <u>Am I doing?</u>: Sto facendo?, <u>Will I do?</u>: Farò?, <u>Have I done?</u>: Ho fatto?, <u>Would I do?</u>: Farei?, <u>Will I be doing?</u>: Starò facendo?, <u>Was I doing?</u>: Stavo facendo?, <u>Do I have to do?</u>: Devo fare?, <u>Have I been doing?</u>: Ho fatto?, <u>Would I have done?</u>: Avrei fatto?, <u>Did I do?</u>: Feci?

Verb <u>*To Work; Lavorare;*</u> <u>Do I work?</u>: Lavoro?, <u>Am I working?</u>: Sto lavorando?, <u>Will I work?</u>: Lavorerò?, <u>Have I worked?</u>: Ho lavorato?, <u>Would I work?</u>: Lavorerei?, <u>Will I be working?</u>: Starò lavorando?, <u>Was I working?</u>: Stavo lavorando?, <u>Do I Have to work?</u>: Devo lavorare?, <u>Have I been working?</u>: Ho lavorato?, <u>Would Have I worked?</u>: Avrei lavorato?, <u>Did I work?</u>: Lavorai?